CROSSING THE RIVER
Poets of the Western U.S.

edited by Ray Gonzalez

The Permanent Press, Sag Harbor, NY 11963

Library of Congress Number: 87-060783
International Standard Book Number: 0-932966-80-2

Manufactured in the United States of America

THE PERMANENT PRESS
RD2 Noyac Road
Sag Harbor, NY 11963

Acknowledgments

PATRICIA GOEDICKE: "For All the Sad Rain" and "After the First Embrace" reprinted from THE WIND OF OUR GOING, Copper Canyon Press. Copyright © 1985 by Patricia Goedicke.

ROBERT BURLINGAME: "Great River in Arid November" appeared in the *Kansas Quarterly*, "Late Walk With A Father" appeared in *Puerto del Sol*, and "Thinking of Fairy Tales" in *The New Jersey Poetry Journal* and TU LU YU IN A LATER AUTUMN, Mesilla Press. Copyright © 1984 Mesilla Press.

LINDA BIERDS: "Pt. Barrow" and "Child in the Wagon" reprinted from OFF THE ALEUTIAN CHAIN, L'Epervier Press. Copyright © 1985 by Linda Bierds.

KEITH WILSON: "The Arrival of My Mother" and "In Sire and Twisted Trees" reprinted from WHILE DANCING FEET SHATTER THE EARTH, Utah State University Press. Copyright © 1978 by Keith Wilson.

WILLIAM PITT ROOT: "Light in a House of Mirrors" reprinted from REASONS FOR GOING IT ON FOOT, Atheneum Publishers. Copyright © 1981 by William Pitt Root and "Blue Lake Dream" from FAULTDANCING, University of Pittsburgh Press. Copyright © 1986 by William Pitt Root.

PAUL ZARZYSKI: "Silos" and "Escorting Grammy" reprinted from THE MAKE-UP OF ICE, University of Georgia Press. Copyright © 1984 by Paul Zarzyski. "Wings" originally appeared in *The Bloomsbury Review*.

JODY ALIESAN: "The Tower," "May Day," and "Spell" reprinted from DESIRE, Empty Bowl. Copyright © 1985 by Jody Aliesan.

NAOMI SHIHAB NYE: "When the Flag is Raised" and "The Man Who Makes Brooms" reprinted from YELLOW GLOVE, Breitenbush Books. Copyright © 1986 by Naomi Shihab Nye.

DAVID ROMTVEDT: "Arson" and "Moon" appeared in the *American Poetry Review* and MOON, Bieler Press. Copyright © 1984 by David Romtvedt.

JACK HEFLIN: "Mules" by Jack Heflin appeared in *The Bloomsbury Review*.

SCOTT DAVIDSON: "Approaching Equinox" appeared in *The New Oregon Review.*
BARBARA LA MORTICELLA: "Truths" and "Horsetail Rush" reprinted from EVEN THE HILLS MOVE IN WAVES, Leaping Mountain Press. Copyright © 1986 by Barbara La Morticella.
PATRICIA DUBRAVA: "April Icon" by Patricia Dubrava appeared in *Breathless Magazine* and "What's It Like In Wyoming" appeared in *Confrontation.*
KARL KOPP: "Ahead the Pacific" by Karl Kopp appeared in *The Bloomsbury Review.*
GRETEL EHRLICH: "A Hawk's Winter Landing" and "Probably She Is A River" reprinted from TO TOUCH THE WATER, Ahsahta Press. Copyright © 1981 by Gretel Ehrlich.
JOHN BRADLEY: "So This Is The World: Biloxi, 1943" by John Bradley appeared in *Puerto del Sol.*
TED KOOSER: "In The Basement of the Goodwill Store," "Abandoned Farmhouse," and "Geronimo's Mirror" reprinted from SURE SIGNS: SELECTED POEMS, University of Pittsburgh Press. Copyright © 1980 by Ted Kooser.
JON DAVIS: "Perfect Landscapes, Rich Branches of Blossom" by Jon Davis appeared in *Cutbank* and "White Body, Green Moss" in *Poetry.*
ALAN CHONG LAU: "Origins" and "A Chinese Landscape Painting in California-18?" reprinted from SONGS FOR JADINA, Greenfield Review Press. Copyright © 1980 by Alan Chong Lau.
LEO ROMERO: "The Moon and Angels," "The Miracle," and "Holy Water" reprinted from CELSO, Arte Publico Press. Copyright © 1986 by Leo Romero.
WENDY BARKER: "Black Sheep, Red Stars" and "The Navy Blue Chair" by Wendy Barker appeared in *Poetry* and "Teeth for Teeth" appeared in *Cedar Rock.*
DEL MARIE ROGERS: "Letter to My Mother" by Del Marie Rogers appeared in *The Bloomsbury Review* and TO THE EARTH, Trilobite Press. Copyright © 1983 by Del Marie Rogers.
ROSEMARY CATACALOS: "Tongue-Tied," "Ariadne to Dionysios" and "Poison In The Eye Of The Beholder"

and "Ricky Ricardo Drinks Alone" reprinted from HOME, Dragon Gate Publishers. Copyright © 1983 by Jim Simmerman. "Then Again" appeared in *Crazy Horse*.

NANCY ANDREWS: "There, Where the Ground Swells" by Nancy Andrews appeared in the *Hampden-Sydney Poetry Review* and "Mine Shaft" appeared in the *Connecticut Poetry Review*.

PAMELA USCHUK: "What You May Have Thought Was Empty" by Pamela Uschuk appeared in *Prickly Pear Poetry Review* and "After Reading Louise Bogan's Journals" appeared in *Poetry*.

MICHAEL SIMMS: "The Blue Heron" and "The Explanation" reprinted from MIGRATION, Breitenbush Books. Copyright © 1985 by Michael Simms. "The Explanation" also appeared in *The Bloomsbury Review*.

WALTER PAVLICH: "On Not Growing Up With Fireflies" reprinted from ONGOING PORTRAITS, Barnwood Press. Copyright © 1985 by Walter Pavlich. "The Albino Raccoon" and "With Eleanor Near the End of a Minus Tide" reprinted from OF THINGS ODD AND THEREFORE BEAUTIFUL, Leaping Mountain Press. Copyright © 1987 by Walter Pavlich.

STANLEY NOYES: "The Dream Painter" and "The Book and the City" reprinted from THE COMMANDER OF DEAD LEAVES, Tooth of Time Books. Copyright © 1985 by Stanley Noyes.

JAMES GRABILL: "An Earthen Night" by James Grabill appeared in *The Chariton Review,* "A Fall" appeared in *The Mid-American Review* and IN THE COILED LIGHT, NRG Press. Copyright © 1984 by James Grabill.

TESS GALLAGHER: "The Kneeling One" reprinted from WILLINGLY, Graywolf Press. Copyright © 1984 by Tess Gallagher.

GENE FRUMPKIN: "Before the Meeting in the World Below" reprinted from NIGHT MUSIC, The Paper. Copyright © 1987 by Gene Frumpkin. "The Metaphysics of Paper" appeared in *The Chariton Review* and "After Reading Some Poems by William Bronk" appeared in *Poetry Northwest*.

FRANK STEWART: "On the Pali Coast, Hawaii," "Above

The editor wishes to thank many friends and supporters for encouragement in completing this book. Among them are Tom and Marilyn Auer, Pat Doyle, Michael Harvey, Bill Broadwell, Peter Ashkenaz, Dale Walker, Pamela Haines, Leslie Baca, Chris Woods, Mike Baehr, Jay Hamburger, Pat Mora, Cindy Miller, Nancy Harrison, Joel Hubbard, Michael Sykes, and most of all, my mother Beatriz Gonzalez, and my sisters—Pat Mena, Susie Terrazas, and Sylvia Post.

This book is dedicated to Richard Hugo, Kenneth Rexroth, and James Wright—in memory and gratitude.

TABLE OF CONTENTS

xi

Crossing the River

Preface

Crossing the River is a collection of poetry from the western United States. I selected the poems because they were written by some of the best poets I know, writers living in the most vital region of the country—the American West. In the last hundred years, no other part of the U.S. has played such a crucial role in shaping its history, but no other place has also been so stereotyped as the region west of the Mississippi River. These poems resonate with the true experience of living in that part of the country.

These poets do away with the stereotype of the cowboy and Indian and write about real people—past and present family, and others who have shaped their lives and influenced the way they interact with their environment. Most important of all, these poets are keen observers of the natural world around them. Their insight has been shaped by three major factors—the freedom to travel and explore, the impact of personal and national history, and the magnetic attraction of the beautiful land.

These forces make the poet a historian whose work has been overlooked when it comes to understanding the western experience. Reading popular biographies on legendary characters and historical accounts of famous events have been traditional ways of learning about the West yet too many of these books romanticize the subject. Historians and sociologists draw conclusions about the story of the country and how it shaped the modern American character, but they ignore a crucial aspect—poetic insight. The poet writing in the West responds with a unique point of view that must be included in the over-all story.

The result is a poetry that allows everyone to find what it is like to live in New Mexico, Texas, Montana, or the Northwest. These poems are able to take us there because they open outward and are not samples of closed "regional" writing that promotes one region over another. They are powerful earth poems that rise out of deserts, plains, mountains, and rivers to celebrate a sense of place that can be found in poets nationwide.

—Ray Gonzalez

PART ONE

Crossing the River

"Today, walking south of the river, I remembered those figures—wide, dusky wings flapping, necks of carved ivory—and I knew that I had seen the birth of a new language"

Jon Davis

PATRICIA GOEDICKE

For All the Sad Rain

O my friends why are we so weak
In winter sunlight why do our knees knock,
Why do we walk with small steps, ugly
And spindly as baby birds

Whose world do we think this is?
O my friends take it,
O my friends don't look at each other
Or anyone else before you speak.

I have had enough of scared field mice
With trembling pink ears,
I have had enough of damp
Diffident handshakes,

Do you think I haven't been stepped on by giants?
Do you think my teachers didn't stand me in a corner
For breathing, do you think my own father
    didn't burn me
With the wrath of a blast furnace for wanting to sit
    on his knee?

Indeed I have been pressed between steamrollers,
I have had both my feet cut off, and the pancreas
And the liver and lungs of the one I love
Have been sucked out of my life and the air around me

Has turned to cereal, how will I stand up,
What opinions can I offer but I will not be silent,
There are dogs who keep their skinny tails
Permanently between their legs

But also there are sleek horses, as easily as there are curs
There are squash blossoms that flower around fountains
Like white butterflies, there is courage everywhere,
For every reluctant nail-biter

There are a hundred raised fists,
    for every broken broomstick
There are millions of bent grasses snapping

3

Back and forth at the sky, beating the blue carpet
As hard as they can, with the frail tassels of their hair

For every pair of eyes squeezed tight
Under colorless lids there are thousands of others
Wide-open, on the proud columns of their necks turning,
Observing everything like King Radar,

O my friends for all the sad rain in heaven
Filling our dinner plates you have ten fingers of honey
Which are your own, stretch them, stick them up
And then, wave to me, put your arms around
   each other's shoulders

When we meet in a field with no fences
The horizon is yours, and the books and all the opinions
And the water which is wine and the best bed
You can possibly think of to lie in.

After the First Embrace

We are separated   almost at once
   From every airport we are calling

As the wash of liquid heat
   Disperses itself   love

Thins out, cooling
   Over the whole globe,

But after the first embrace
   In Sacramento there will be one pocket,
      Here and there others,

A few cooking fires   friends
   That still remain to us   flickering
      Just over the lip of earth,

Gathered around the hearth signaling
   Greetings from nowhere
      Touchable. . .

As the messages come back, jittering
    Over the torn wires

Lying in bed, I listen
    To the tapes they send, spoken

Days past: the children
    Fly back and forth, believers

They grow tomatoes, bread
    Rises   in small ovens,

Thread knots itself into islands
    Clusters of people waving

For the lacework of our lives
    Is so fragile, by day

From East to West fingertips
    Ravel, reach for each other. . .

But talking all night like candles
    In the windows of the young

Though we gutter out by morning
    In Mexico, China, Greece,
        Each face cannot be present

Every minute   where are you
    Though the fabric rots   the pain

Holds us together   here
    In Cuba, Alaska, New Zealand

Fire shoots across the heavens,
    Or falls in the water, stunned

Tongues speak, burning
    Chunks of meterorites whose absence

Is not absence   in this life waking
    In darkness   I hear your voices

We who are one body
    We who are one body.

ROBERT BURLINGAME

Great River In Arid November

This cloudless morning we walk into the river's
Bed sucked dry to its middle by November drought.
Only the ripple marks, rounded scars of old flows,
Announce that deep water raged here once.
The waved and scalloped sand shines like a small Sahara.
It tells secrets about the furious underbelly
Of melting snow and how it swirled silt to shape—
Rain-rasped from shoulders of Colorado rock.

Everywhere smooth disdainless mounds
   and valleys cradle
And seduce the light. All is bleached and frail.
All is order shaped by formlessness—brittle peace
Lapped and havened beneath the sun's bland watch.
And yet so much perfection—and poise—disconcerts.
The very stillness says "no wet, no life." Far off,
High, we hear the cronks of equatorial geese
And begin to wish this way might suddenly roar
With spring. The prim sandy scrolls beg savage birth.

But to be drowned to life is a fearful thing.
So quickly we turn toward the grassy bank, climb
Back into our world of fixed stumps and cracks. Then we
Look down once more and pray this dried pelvic place,
Earth's lavish cup, will fill again, but stay its course.

Thinking Of Fairy Tales

We read them still.
When we do they are good enough
to keep us awake,
these mouths of all beginning.

6

What is it?
What is it exactly that they hold for us,
even when we've crumbled into bland adults?

We would have to look into some pool
into the pure center
of its deepest
dark
    to find an answer.
It would come as a fish, as an ugly head,
as a contrary mote of light.
We would have to take the fairy tale test
of admitting we are helplessly big.
We would have to stoop down to the littleness
    of the polliwog.

It is hard to see our life as shambles or pit.
It is hard to find "the prettiest girl that ever was"
    is the soul we've airily aborted.
It is hard to recognize the "kind king" as the son
    we've slaughtered.

Late Walk With A Father

My father appears at the door.
And asks, "How are you, son?"
Evening's wind jokes with his thin hair.
He has the look of a vague star,
        the voice of a dreaming tree.
"I'm all right," I tell him.
"And you, are your fields still drunk with sunflowers?"
He smiles. "No, they're all quiet now."

He comes with the evening into my room.
Watches me with his two different eyes.
Then says, "How about that hike in the hills?"
I stare into his right eye
a coldness in it,
        the silence of the owl's swoop.

7

We walk out but I can't think what to say.
All I can remember is my mother undressing.

LINDA BIERDS

Pt. Barrow

She was lactating. We know this
by the right, swollen breast.
By the swollen bladder, the lank stomach,
we know it was early morning.

So the hours become these hours.

An Arctic storm, rare in the springtime,
scales sod from a dome
fattened
by the amber, marrow-filled bones of the gray whale.
Beneath it, a woman,
a man and small child are sleeping.
The dome is made humid by a circular flame of moss,
sputtering in the throat of a seal-lamp.
In its blinking, flip-frame light, the sleepers,
the arrows and buckets,
appear, disappear.

It is 1600.

The woman wakes to a yawl of cracking whalebones.
At the beach below her shelter, the on-shore wind,
the flood-tide, the sea-ice melting for weeks

combine in a statement of preservation.

Nothing in her world has sounded like this, has
pressed like this. She is lifted,
tasting salt. Slowly, her stiffened walrus blanket
leaves ridges on her buttocks.

We trace them.

We trace the ragged blossoms of seal-smoke
blackening her lungs.

There is sperm stalled at the lip of her cervix.
And here,

on her shoulder,
a dozen shallow trenches, scratched
by the ornamental claws of a walrus blanket, that

chafed, chafed,
that, just before midnight, rolled off

with her spent husband, like
a black bear, comic, mottled with light.

Surely, she spoke then. Surely

the child, keeping sleep, took
her language to a dream, gave it
motion, shape,
hurled its icy, perfect body into the hours.

Child in the Wagon

The child in the wagon remembers a sound:
leaves that clicked down the cobblestones
like the toenails of running dogs.
It was evening. She turned, expecting the worst,
and found instead the swirl of madrona leaves
and then on the street corner
candleflames cupped in their glass boxes.

I will not hear that sound again, she thinks,
and looks to her left, right,
where the long Conestoga wagons bumble
through the switchgrass. There are forty, indigo
and red, moving not single file but *abreast,*
their hoops and canvas hoods swaying white, and
seen from above, the child thinks, like a wave

9

spilling into the harbor, its line of froth
and the dust swelled up behind like a second wave.

So the pattern continues, until day ends
and the center wagons stall, all their horses
simply stepping in place as the end wagons
arc toward one another and the wagoners
on their lazyboards draw up
their perfect circle, like the nets of Maine fishermen.
That evening, near sleep on the floorboards,
the child describes to her parents
the sound of madrona leaves, running dogs.
How, for an instant, fear passed through her
like an icy tooth—the long-haired sea dogs
rushing in from the ships—
and then there was nothing: leaves, a certain peace.

And that sound . . . like this? her mother whispers,
clicking knives to a pewter cup. Then the father—
who will die in October, his cheeks in miniature
the caved salt cliffs they are leaving—
begins, tapping this, that, this, that,
until the wagon, in its circle of wagons, fills.
And there on the canvas, the child thinks,
how beautiful the hand shadows are:
great moths come in from the wilderness.
Like this? they ask. Like this?
As if in a moment, the absolute sound
might appear—then the dogs rush past, thick with loss.
And there would be peace.

KEITH WILSON

The Arrival of My Mother

—*New Mexico Territory, 1906*

She got off, according to her diary,
dressed in a lovely beaded gown, fresh
from Washington with sixteen trunks of ballgowns,
chemises, blouses (4 Middie), shoes and assorted
lingerie. She was at that time about 25, old
for an unmarried woman. Her stiff mother was at
her side, she also wildly overdressed for New Mexico
sun and wind.

What must she have thought, seeing my uncle standing,
hat in hand in the dust of that lonely train house,
cracked yellow paint, faded letters of welcome
for passengers that rarely come?

The buckboard was waiting and they rode out into
the darkness of evening toward the tent, & that half
built frame homestead house, wind dying as the sun
sank, birdcries stilled.

I see her now outshooting my father and me, laughing
at our pride and embarrassment. My sister, as good a
shot, waiting her turn. Or that picture of her
on horseback, in Eastern riding clothes beside the Pecos.
A picnic when I was small and how my father lifted me up
to her and she carefully walked the horse around rock
and sand.

        I suppose she finally arrived in New Mexico
in the April of one year when my sister and I sat beside
a rented bed, each holding one of her hands and watched
her eyes grow childlike, unmasked as a *kachina*
entering the final *kiva* of this dance. The old mother
heavy with years slipped away and the woods of New
England dimmed as these dry hills ripened and caught

11

her last breath, drums, drums should have sounded
for the arrival of my mother.

In Sere & Twisted Trees

—El Rito, New Mexico

Walking the small trails of stonecropped hills,
my son and I read with the grains of our skins
the old language, its tongues of night and day,
toned winds and the watching trees and skies.

How it all grows easy and secure when one realizes
everything is alive in the summer's sun, listening
watching. I speak to my brothers. I tell them
we are coming, meaning no harm. Wait. My son, 10,
is a fisherman, and he hopes to catch trout.
I tell them this, promise he will eat what he catches.
I will see to this.

                    A prayer for the trout.
A prayer for my son, whom I love more than ever
watching his graceful figure dance to the rod
and fly he made. I needn't have bothered the trout.
He was wiser than my son. We walk back, Kevin,
still excited, apparently not caring about the lack
of fish, full of the adventure of the day.

He no longer holds my hand now, and I understand.
His embraces are quick, embarrassed, his eyes
shifting warily away towards the hills. It won't
be long, as this canyon's time is measured,
before he leaves me. Pray for me, Trout.
Pray for me, Mountain Stream.

JOHN BRANDI

There is This You, This Me

There is a net between your breasts
a net of deep sighs & fields mowed with blades of steel.
There is an owl who flies over you
an owl whose eyes bleed & who never remembers names.
There is an ear at your side, an ear that hears
whispers of other lovers
who've come to you on mornings like these.

There is soil between your teeth
soil of buried seeds & vanished towns, of hidden
letters & deaths of ones near.
There is a highway that connects us
a highway through trample of rain
& mirrored canyons at the break of day.

There is this you, this me
who fold into the deepest blossom
with no fear of night's undertow, no dark hedge
behind which to pretend.

There is a river of dust, a mirage
of silence to begin the world.
There is your face & mine.
There are these bodies never here for long
these breasts & private parts ready to sing.
This innocence, this lust
this pain we hold.

There is this you, this me
who sleep inside shadows, who rise
from under a wing, to grasp a hand through a flame
& discover Someone waiting, whose flesh
reveals the Body inside the bodies of everyone.

Hymn for a Night Feast

Take the war from me.
Take the penumbra for a crossroad.
Make a parachute from our bedsheets.
Run your hand across the circuit of air
stirred by our bodies.

Take the right and wrong from me.
Take the gleam in the Lamb's eye
and wear it as a gown.
Our flesh is counterfeit.
Fire douses water.
Flame spreads the wind.

Take the smoke from my garden.
Take the river as extreme unction.
This room is moist with praise.
A crane lifts its wings
under a canopy of filtered light.

Take what is left and rock the sea.
Take the firefly, the hour hand, the iris.
Make me glorious to the world again.
Give me courage to ask
your name.

WILLIAM PITT ROOT

Light In A House Of Mirrors

considerations at La Push

"Islands high as our inland hills"
—John Logan

1

I sleep deep in a clump of dark humped trees
where the river forks and roars below a bridge.

14

I sleep fitful as light in a house of mirrors,
dream of a drunken Indian
who sells me my own scalp slick as a skinned cat, dripping.

   But when I wake and write to a friend
the dream I tell for her
is of a shape like my shape by the river,
filling slowly with a sunlight
bright as honey, quick as rain.
A tall attentive glow beside dark water.

2

Here were the flatfaced people whose earthfathers
circled toward
this land over a blue idea
of godliness
melting behind them, burning before.

3

The flatfaced stones beneath my feet
predate Cezanne
longer than 10,000 redwoods end-to-end have lived
swallowing air and sunlight, rain and drifting
soil up into that gradual dance of the self
in whose shadow even longlived tortoise withers—

Split and fracture,
                  dark falls of light
squaring edges of the once-round stone.

Scald and freeze of passion's glance and intellect's regard.

4

A great ghoul grey from the ruin of a log
rose like mist before me
as I took my last steps back to camp, startling
as if to distract me from my story.
                              But no,
it was only my imagination, yellow-eyed and moss-faced
again.

15

5

Once there was more land, higher than now. The
waters grew jealous, gathered their tribes and con-
spired. Men knew this and the greatest planned to
flee inland, leaving the others—the sickly and the
weak—to form a wall to hold back the waters. So
there they stood, and the waters were delayed before they rushed inland. Today we can see the
heads of the old ones at the shore here, vast, moss-
haired, silent—for these were the runts, the least of
their race—and we feel dwarfed beside them. For
the greatfathers, who were saved, shrivelled among
the safe places far inland. The heroes still stand
guard at the edges. We call them stones so we will
not remember. They no longer speak to us, who
are neither their sons or daughters.

Blue Lake Dream

1.
I float upon a lake, suspended
In my simple boat of skin.

All above me is the azure
Blazing of the inner bowl.

Below and all around
Extends the mirror, tense and blue.

I am floating on my back,
Arms spread, legs parallel, eyes wide.

2.
I am drawn swirling upward
By the vacuum of the dome,

Rushing downward by the massive depths:
Slowly on the surface I revolve.

All around the great blue
Mountains of the shore

Ring me with increasing force,
Pull with power absolute

And absolutely countered
By the magnet of my heart.

Between explosion outward
And collapse within

I am witness
To the awe of stasis,

I, who am Lodestone,
I, Brain,

I, inner sun
Utterly ablaze in the ark of the Skull.

3.
Floating on my back I am turning
As Earth turns—flung out from the center,

Drawn in by the core—,
Arms spread, eyes wide.

Eyes gone blind as stone.
Eyes made clear as diamond.

4.
In my skull grows
A light

Brighter than all the fire
Round Salamander's hull

Who sets forth through the wavering of flames
Who will not dwell in fire

Who shall pass through.

PAUL ZARZYSKI

Silos

against Augusta, Montana: prairie dovetailed
with Rockies, raptor with hard wind, hard
grass and grain, with cattle and antelope
with Flat Creek—rainbow,
brown and brook trout—with buckbrush
coulee—jack rabbit and mule deer—
with snowberry, cocklebur and rosehip scrub
—Hungarian partridge and sharptail—
with sun and moon with Tabletop
and Steamboat Mountain, with Haystack
Butte, Gobblers' Knob, Bean Lake, and yardlight
to yardlight, that distant dark we love
between stars. Silos against Augusta:
honeybee with Hutterite with family ranch—
the Minuteman launching pads
against everything from Dearborn River
to jackfence to cowhorse and combine
rolling with the camber and cant, rolling
with the land. Ballistic Missile vaults
square off in a chain all their own
against the horizontal grain
of glacier and age: warheads
from Augusta, from earth still festering
cavalry repeating carbines
to the surface—shrapnel
through old scars—where cattle stir,
moon to salt lick to moon,
this veteran wind
once bulletproof, this distance
no longer dark, no longer living
out of sight and range.

Wings

I clench his feathered legs together
like a jilted suitor clings
to a limp bouquet. All his love
nocturnal, in a nightmareless life,
he could not foresee, even with ball-
turret vision, the existence of so much
sterile light and steel: this Great
Gray Owl in shock, deflated,
on a veterinary table, one wing-
bone, jagged as glass pipette,
broken in two.
                              His eyes, dull bulbs
to the brilliance of this room,
beam nothing of his ominous lore,
his fury at our pluck and probe. Humiliation
quells his outrage for mangled plumes
he'd preened quill by quill
to perfection—each barbule
softly muffling the owl's swoop—this ruffled
breadth of feathers that hid his frailness
for so little flesh.
                              The vet threads
a metal pin into the shattered
miracle of air-as-marrow, little hope
hollow bone will knit at all, let alone
knit with struts enough for flight. The owl,
shocked and marred, wilted
by so much light, leaves his body
to our last-ditch, taxidermic bid
for immortality. We'll never know
what secret love, what spirit locked within
quill and bone, kept this bird
eternally in blossom—crest feathers
petaled like phlox, ten thousand wings
soaring gorgeous for the dark.

Escorting Grammy to the Potluck Rocky Mountain Oyster Feed at Bowman's Corner

—for Ethel "Grammy" Bean

Lean Ray Krone bellers through a fat cumulus
cloud of Rum-Soaked Wagonmaster Conestoga
Stogie smoke he blows across the room,
"They travel in 2's, so better eat them even
boys, or kiss good luck good-bye for good."

Tonight the calf nuts, beer batter-dipped
by the hundreds, come heaped
and steaming on 2-by-3 foot trays
from the kitchen—deep-fat fryers
crackling like irons searing hide.

And each family, ranching Augusta
Flat Creek country, brings its own brand
of sourdough hardrolls, beans, gelatins,
slaws and sauces, custard and mincemeat
pies to partner-up to the main chuck.

At the bar, a puncher grabs a cow-
poxed handful—7 of the little buggers—
feeding them like pistachios
from palm to pinch fingers to flick-
of-the-wrist toss on target.

Grammy, a spring filly at 86, sips
a whisky-ditch in one hand, scoops
the crispy nuggets to her platter
with the other, forks a couple
and goes on talking Hereford Bulls.

And me, a real greenhorn to this cowboy
caviar—I take to them like a pup
to a hoof paring, a porky
to a lathered saddle, a packrat
to a snoosebox full of silver rivets.

I skip the trimmings, save every cubic inch
of plate and belly for these kernels,

20

tender nubbins I chew and chew till the last
pair, left for luck, nuzzle on the tray
like a skylined brace of round bales.

A cattleland Saturday grand time with Grammy
is chowing down on prairie pecans, then driving
the dark-as-the-inside-of-a-cow grangehall
trail home to dream heifer-fat, bull-necked
happy dreams all night long in my Sunday boots.

JODY ALIESAN

The Tower

> "... *the frog-shaped Heqet* ... *primordial mother
> of all existence, which she generates and
> protects.*"

Erich Neumann, *The Great Mother*

toads called spadefoot survived
slow drying of the southwest sea
now new mexico learned to dig
sometimes fifteen feet down stay
weeks at a time

        once a road crew found
under old concrete in a baked clay ball
one of them still alive

        eyes cat slits
they surface to eat only at night
instead of breeding in spring they mate
whenever it rains

        night before trinity
what oppenheimer named first

21

bomb test after donne's holy sonnet
batter my heart three person'd god
thunderstorm over ground zero

lightning near the tower

                         before dawn
in the bunkers six miles away they heard
spadefoot song loudest among toads and frogs
hurry I've found water to mate in

hundreds moving mounting leaving
moonstone clouds on the sand wet
still enough for tadpoles maybe
long enough for them to turn

sunrise man announcing countdown
loudspeakers over trenches wondered
microphone in his hand *would it*
somewhere between five and four
electrocute him if he held it spoke
ONE threw it to the floor screamed

        ZERO

between his scream and the bloom of death
only sound was the toads' singing

May Day *(with thanks to H. G. Wells)*

> *"being a perfectionist and being scared
> are often the same thing"*
>
> John Fowles

I crash through brambles every time
into the same clearing
someone hold me stroke me rock me
until I fall asleep until morning

god has no thighs when I cry
out to him in the night

he doesn't turn over and ask
is something the matter

wild animals give everything to fate
but they still move away from what hurts

before it scalds hot water feels cool
only when sweat rushes from organs to skin
do I reel blind throw up
hands eyes wade into the sound
without stopping prairie child
never seen anything taller than creeks
thrown into deep end swimming pool
life erupting in green chlorine bubbles

after we saw whales she asked *did you cry*
as I get older I cry more easily

every spring clawing up cedar roots
hacking back ivy blackberry vines
they want to take over I'm tired
of struggling I want someone to tell me
what's best for me I feel like giving up

wonderful she said *that's progress*
how long can this go on
don't lose your nerve

Spell

let the woodworker's hands broad and smooth
twining veins on a lattice of tendons
lift your leg like the neck of a cello

let the one who strokes feathers from paper
with the brush of his fingertips draw
your lips and the nipple of your fiercest

> quickening you must
> press his face away his
> slightest breathing is
> too much to bear

23

let the sculptor's hands burnish and strew
your bronze sand into the furnace
ground oyster shell fanned under birds

fall down on the field-quilted waters
his bone-nosed eagle his knee-bent
stallion his hanging fish will find you

NAOMI SHIHAB NYE

When the Flag is Raised

For Judith McPheron

Today the vein of sadness pumps
its blue wisdom through this room and
you answer with curtains. A curtain lifts
and holds itself aloft.

Somewhere in Texas, a motel advertises
rooms for "A Day, Week, Month, or Forever."
The melancholia of this invitation
dogs me for miles.
Sometimes I lie in bed reading biographies,
traveling one paragraph three times
to feel its graceful turns and glides.
Naturally all other lives feel
more solid and trustworthy
than any life right in front of me
which is the great stupidness
of my kind of animal.
Nothing is ever the same because
no one else is either.
I go to the sink, splash water on my face.
In the morning sailors in sailor suits
park their cars in front of my house

and march around the block.
It is like we live on different shores.

More than anything I honor how some voices
raise a flag, even if the sinking country
will not stay whole. When we reconsider
our own vanishing measures of air,
when the great loser of the heart
subtracts another odyssey, stitching itself
a new garment of pink skin,
the flag is above us, waving without urgency,
waving like the word "remember"
triggers the tongue.

I will remember how I woke with your voice
filtering other voices, steadily penetrating
the walls, saying, *Traveler,* saying, *Take Note,*
so I was packing the small bag from the beginning again
as if anyone could use it.
Now it was breath and needle,
the impeccable fine print of leaves.
We were leaving the grip of silence behind us.
There were so many people we needed to see.

The Man Who Makes Brooms

So you come with these maps in your head
and I come with voices chiding me to
"speak for my people"
and we march around like guardians of memory
till we find the man on the short stool
who makes brooms.

Thumb over thumb, straw over straw,
he will not look at us.
In his stony corner there is barely room
for baskets and thread,
much less the weight of our faces
staring at him from the street.
What he has lost or not lost is his secret.

25

You say he is like all the men,
the man who sells pistachios,
the man who rolls the rugs.
Older now, you find holiness in anything
that continues, dream after dream.
I say he is like nobody,
the pink seam he weaves
across the flat golden face of this broom
is its own shrine, and forget about the tears.

In the village the uncles will raise their *kefiyahs*
from dominoes to say, no brooms in America?
And the girls who stoop to sweep the courtyard
will stop for a moment and cock their heads.
It is a little song, this thumb over thumb,
but sometimes when you wait years
for the air to break open
and sense to fall out,
it may be the only one.

The Silence of Hutchinson, Kansas:
A Letter From Texas

All night the Queen's Crown
unwraps fat heart-shaped leaves,
sticky tendrils curling
in the holes of each screen.
We wake to find it halfway
up the house.

Each day the gray fluted plate
from Hutchinson dries quietly
in the rack. Two women who saved it,
who sold it to me, were selling
the salt shakers of fifty years,
the cowboy, the chef,
the porcelain bride.
They would not smile
for anyone. Later I stood

26

on the steps of their house
where the sound of fences
and yards rolling forward
held me in its fist.
You stood, and the dog
behind a bush never saw us,
he was sleeping so hard.

I could have said, your life
is here. For years and years
the bricks of your house
had stuck together and people
of your street had gone to work
and come home. It was so silent
each morning after they left
we wore their shoes
from room to room. I could have said,
hold out your hand.

What was it we waited for,
standing on those steps,
pausing at the rim of
so many lives?
Once in the library, we lost
each other among the shelves.
I knew you have read every one
of those books and felt terrified
by their spines.

Now I would say how
every song has a blank in it.
I would pause again, to listen.
Envelopes arrive from St. Louis,
Mexico, but never from
the land of wheat.
I would say we said everything
once, long ago, but know it is only
distance welding its shiny crown,
tilting its head.
And the root of silence
which adheres a little deeper each day
is the only thread connecting me

to a town I once entered
and exited by road.

DAVID ROMTVEDT

Arson

At work we found a rattler.
The job was to make a rip-rap
on the desert as if waves
would someday reach that sea. But it was
only to stop erosion so men could stand on artificial
mounds to fire their guns across the air. I don't
remember thinking the snake would strike. I can't
remember any fear or idea that I wanted
to take action. I didn't say a word when another boy
said, "We have to kill it." and no one disagreed. So we
did it with stones, at the end striking its head
like hammering nails to hold targets, hanging
on to the stone. Then an older man slit its belly
open, throat to tail, telling stories about other rattlers,
scrambled eggs and snake brains, being alone
on the desert. He uncoiled nine unborn snakes, eyes
still creamlike membrane. They tried to wind themselves
back round, moving from side to side. It may be they
were alive or if not, all tropism, some dead creature's
dance of nerve endings and light. I must not have asked,
must not have said a thing, just
looked, learning that rattlesnakes are born
one at a time: the unwinding of the young
on the flat surface of a stone
where they sizzle and pop in the faultless sun.

Moon

If you are a man
who loves women please now look
at the nipples of the woman you love.
Turn to her in this very moment and begin.
Do you think a poet or anyone else
for that matter can say that a nipple
is somehow like a moon, say that
nipples swell and rise like dark moons?
I think not. Nothing is really like
nothing else. In beginning
some of you will want to tear her shirt open.
I will say to nonviolently unbutton
her shirt but that is my personality.

Look at her round nipples. If your lover
is not here or if you have no lover ask
the woman seated nearest you if she would
like you to look at her nipples. She may
say no. Do not press the issue, perhaps
you will sneak a glance when she doesn't see.

If you are a woman
who loves women look at your female
lover's nipples. Ask her to look
simultaneously at your own. You will
notice each others' breasts. Let your
four nipples touch. Do not think
the four breasts are any more four moons
than your four nipples. You may be envious
of your lover's large breasts if they are large
or of her smaller breasts if they are that.
Remember we are here addressing nipples
so do not let breasts distract your attention.

The two of you can look at each other in mirrors
or upside down or in showers. If you are now
beginning to show your nipples to your lover
please do not be angry with the lonely man
who sneaks a glance your way.

    If you are a woman
who loves men that too is alright. You
can look at your own nipples or you can
look at the man you love as he looks
at your nipples or you can look at
the man's nipples for they will harden
and rise. And just as your nipples are not
like moons so his are not at all
like cold nickles and dimes.

If by some sad and cruel blow of fate
your male lover has no nipples and you are disgusted
by the narcissistic pleasure of yourself you may
go and look at the moon rising, trying
to look only at the moon. Now I have come to that
for which some of you have been waiting.

    If you are a man
who loves men, you who some will call
cursed, who in some way many do not
understand are blessed, you too must now
open your shirts to each other groping along
in the way you do. Like everyone else
you have no parts like moons, you are, of course,
nothing like nothing else. We are all here
together now, I hope, with our shirts in our hands.

JACK HEFLIN

Good News

Somewhere north of Redwing, Minnesota
our train bridges a snow-crusted secret
whose waters go unspoken till spring.
Ahead, the tracks lead over a marshland
and above the bluffs

I watch a last shield of sunlight
break into roses over the frozen cushions
of cattails dimpled with snow.
An eagle, dreaming of spangled trout,
floats southward on a freezing wind.

As if it had been waiting all day
darkness wades into the valley
delivering the same moon,
though tonight it is only the torn edge
of an envelope that one has opened
and read good news.

I've talked to no one for twelve hours
but if I spoke now, I could say nothing wrong.
Huddled around red fires lighting the river,
the shadows of fishermen grow into
the shadow of forest back of the ice.
Curled and rocking I listen to the low talk
of the mother and child behind me. Her voice
is the snow thrown upward past my window.
It's not a bird, love, it's the moon.

The Treasure of the Raccoons

When I tripped the sack spilled twenty pounds of coon:
the dead and the dead drunk eye to eye.
Some nights lost like this
we'd scared a flock of dozing turkeys,
or that couple from Bollinger County
Roscoe caught screwing over a corvair hood.
But there was one night we come upon
    some Indian graves,
like mossy wens, out near Sophie Layton's.
And Butch was hell to dig into one.

                    In his dream
the Indians told old man Layton of silver.
For fifteen years he cracked his back
inside the limestone holes he'd dug,

31

his creek bottoms gone headhigh in weeds.
One day the dream ran out, the dream
which couldn't find the silver of his wedding ring
lost years before. He died looking up to daylight
he could not climb to.

Now Butch, bent for treasure, a foot and a half down,
digging with the butt of his 22, I say
Butch, let it go, let's get them dogs.
                                    Hold it,
he says. We turn our flashlights on the drunken blur
of a child's foot webbed in mud and flint.
And the dogs, suddenly come up unnoticed in the wind,
let go howls ringed wiht a little of that silver
we'll all find at the bottom of our graves.

Mules

Near the tobacco barns
and red-graveled roads
where my father grew up
in western Kentucky
the mules begin to lose their teeth
and they gather around the rusted plows
and wait unharnessed. This morning
someone points at them from a car window
and disappears
down a county road
that leads to the trellised porches
where old relatives
squint across their jonquilled yards.

I am a long way from home.
I think I may be the man
who tugged at their halters
each morning before dawn.
If I call their names
they will know.

GEORGE KALAMARAS

Across a Thousand Acres of Clouds

for Steve Schmid in Toluca, Mexico

The sun slants
through the cottonwood,
here in Colorado, grazing
dark brown leaf-buds.
Then it pulls back, combing the foothills
in one slow arc, where ants touch
the new light of an overturned log
in a ditch, following the spiral of the sun
as it coils deep inside
its fallen grain, dragging the light
of this town far back
into its fossil home.

And in Mexico,
the trees are full of this same light,
or full of rain. Sometimes I see
the sun hovering like a ghost
of the rain, far up, in a cloud, glowing
inside each drop of water.

Maybe the old Greeks were right.
Maybe tiny humans breathe inside each drop of sperm,
the way the sun swims inside each raindrop,
diving like gray fish, plunging
past screen doors and windowpanes,
through the dust and sweat of small towns.

Maybe it is the sun inside
this rain that makes the rocks
glow at night. Moonlight that moves
again over dark oceans, rising
in silver strands of seaweed, the husband
alone in watery lamplight, fingering

the table's faded blond grain
when he returns home, finally. The new mother
holding her infant, as he reaches from under her
raincoat, grasping for a single drop of sunlight
in the early mist
that combs the foothills.

                                    And the other
light, paint chipping with each sudden turn
of wind, the light of alleys
and crippled bars, the amber light
that dazzles the rim of the shot-glass,
smoke twisting off the cigarette
of the guy who wipes tables
in the back room of the Hotel Mohawk,
the lamp across the street
insects swarm around like black smoke,
the purple light hissing below
the metal hum of traffic, the green light
on the rusty panel of the press operator
who works all night
in the false light of the brickyard,
the hungry light of so many workers
returning home from graveyard shifts
in The Harbor, throats rasping
from too many cigarettes
and the chemical dust again
on their handkerchiefs.

                                    And yes now,
it has begun to rain, damp insects
fall around me like broken wedges
of night; down the foothills
bits of darkness creep; shadows lift
and spin off in clouds.

In Mexico, rain
floods the southern plain, beading up
on flat, clay roofs of cantinas, signs creaking
their metal bodies, doors slamming
in sweeping gusts that shag hungry workers
home from fields.

It is with this wind
I feel the other light at times, a panther
prowling through thin leaves
of the blood. It is a pupil of black light
that opens so wide I could fly through,
fly back through this rain, back
to the people of dust and shadow,
to the pale light of lovers
who on December's solstice do not touch,
and beneath them, to a shadow
growing restless in the dirt,
and down further, near the red light
that rises in the coals
of the winter fire.

Song for the Father

This hole, this dark coat I slip inside and
    drag around is an immense sadness.
The dark wells are filling with rain, my Father,
    and their sadness, filling the sleeves of this
    coat, this sack of badger-blood that spills and
    bloats the open chalice of leaves, the silk
    handkerchief tucked inside the breast pocket
    of your Sunday suit, a sudden kiss.

I would give all the rain of the wells
    to touch you again, once, briefly, while you're
    still young.
There—by accident—beneath the red circle of steam
    rising under the winter street-lamp, to walk
    right up to you in the open, without knowing
    you, in another life perhaps, where we never met,
    but feel hard with our bones maybe somewhere we
    have, to brush the sleeve of your coat with my
    heavy body and sip the vinegar of the heart
    we both threw away to the dogs.

There is still so much of us
  circling the hair-dust, luminous tongues of
  the earth-heart.
And yes, sometimes I do hate you and want you gone
  like the smell of a bad lie I told the woman
  that first spring beneath lilacs, or the panther's
  slow kiss of snow, or money maybe, but greener,
  a sad thing howling from the iron door of a locket.

This hole, this coat I wear, this immense hole
  is a sadness sadder than a kite folding into
  a fire.
It is the sudden shiver in maples in autumn, the stiff
  enamel kiss they lower deep into the earth and keep
  lowering into the hungry soil of our bones, a
  handkerchief, tucked with perfect corners, a single
  piece of embroidered silk that will not untwist
  itself, a dark rain I would bury in the wells
  if I only could, if only my hands were free and
  not clutching this simple kiss the sun hung
  in the air, a gray bell in the breath between us,
  between these years, that Sunday.

STEVE SANFIELD

The Heat

All day
following the cat
—the coolest spots.

Too hot to eat
but still
I stay fat.

Chickens and rabbits
die in the valley.
We face another day.

Horny
but far too hot
to do anything about it.

After two weeks
no remembrance of anything
but the heat.

The heat
makes everything still
except my heart.

A cooling
and the work
leaps forward.

Guest and Host Are Clearly Distinguishable

Went to see Old Bill yesterday
Filled with humble pie I told him
how we stopped to help a turtle
across Tyler Road.

"Knew a fella' once
Lived over in San Juan
Folks called him Lucky
One day he stopped to help
a turtle across the road
Got run down by a loggin truck
They gave him a fancy funeral
But you'd best be careful."

True nature is clear and obvious
Just don't ask for an explanation.

A Cycle of Hoops for the First Snow

Waking this morning
to find the world
covered in white.

The brown grasses
seen afresh
after a night of snow.

Even that junkpile
I meant to put in order
is perfect.

Going outside
just to make a hole
by pissing in the snow.

Limbs cracking.
Branches snapping.
Snow doing its work.

Melting snow
falling from the oaks—
the days of my life.

On moonlight snow
even my shadow
is cold.

Tracks in the snow:
what happened
while we've slept.

The power of snow
to make all things
new.

SANDRA ALCOSSER

Fox Fire

Once, I thought we would know everything,
that's what this was for, this fox fire,
this fragrant energy like nighthawks
screaming at dusk.

All winter I stalked elk that were down
from the mountain and starving.

38

I walked the low places where they galloped
through slush, the rocks where they wallowed
and pawed for new grasses, the tooth marks
on aspen, the mineral lick, the creek
where the water was roiled and milky.
I sweated through immovable snow
and fell down exhausted, but when I imagined
I'd stand in a thicket, my eyes glazed over,
my sharp breath, and know the cold
communion of elk, I was wrong.

Once I thought we were all gods
blessed and strutting this lovely planet.
The earth was a minor passing, like the path
down to our ditch for water, pretty
with serviceberry, but transient.
As a young girl I swung upside down
with other girls as we hung by our heels
from a jungle gym and contemplated heaven.
It was a silky place. I preferred
purgatory, like a dark cafe,
retrievers curled about the table legs
and the warm abraded doors.

At thirty-eight I'm still the babe
of my family. Once I thought they would teach me,
that even their last breath would be a key,
but now I see them drifting off from their easy chairs,
like a tribe leaving shore together, the television
blaring, their mouths sagged open, and when they
return for brief moments, they stare at me
as if I were a stranger.

All that I will ever know is right here
in the wash and till of my own ten acres.
Frost tonight and behind it the whole summer
so brief I can still see the bronco-faced calf
born to the bloody pasture and the brown trout
suspended in its first glittering insect hatch.
There will never be more than twilight, a valley
receding to glass. In this tiny paradise
of common flowers, the waist-high marigolds

blaze up like golden dowagers. Venus rises alone
and early to a cold black sky.

The Entomologist's Landscape

"I go the circuit of my enclosure over and over again"
—Henri Fabre

He picks through the couchgrass, here a black-eared
chat on its nest of blue eggs, and there in the red clay
a natterjack bathes its wary back. Henri crouches,
like a scarab in his yellow jacket, and waits.

His son, Little Paul, keeps a birdcage full
   of peacock moths,
all male. Downstairs a female slips off her pale cocoon
and stands shivering. Wet fur, maroon and white.
On her wings, enormous chestnut eyes. Henri carries her
in a bell jar from room to room. At night
   he and Little Paul
turn the suitors loose. They storm through the cypress
to the laboratory where they beat against
the white gauze bell.

When the bait is right, anything can find you.
I look across the river this morning
   where last I saw a grizzly
batting swollen salmon. A large man stands in a thicket
of raspberries, waving. He wears a tweed jacket
and patent leather boots. Perhaps it is
   the cottonwood bud
I smashed, dabbed behind my ear like bloody perfume.

Mother's gone off to Maine in search of a secret island.
She will gather lobster, rub their green bellies
   so they hum
as they enter boiling water. On the leeward side
she will meet a Rockefeller who mows his own
boulder-dense lawn. If I stay in one place too long,

grow my hair like a banner, and for the hummingbirds,
hang out a red begonia, whose secret island will I be?

Other than the muscular man, only one person comes.
An old painter with a reducing lense, she grades
the landscape: the mountains are a bookcase
full of shale and lichen, the trapezoidal lightning,
the air that tastes of grape jam. By all standards,
she says, we are sublime.

I myself prefer small scenes. I would have liked Henri.
We could have spent the day together
    on our hands and knees,
year after year the same weedlot,
    studying the digger wasp
as she squeezed a wild bee to her breast, then turned
to lick honey from its gasping tongue.

Each Bone A Prayer

Your letters arrive frail from Nepal:
stamps of antelope and monkey-dancers, laughing
though they have not seen fruit in days.

Outside Manang women watch you.
A nomad wearing dangling jade
waves you into her tent. From her hands
you take a bowl of yak milk. Delicious.
You would remain, but the sky
already rots with water.

Crossing the path at Thorong La, your brain
begins to swell. You sleep in the arms
of a sherpa who feeds you opium, picks
leeches from your body. You would die,
but the rain is too lonely.

In the valley his family touches your chest,
the curly black hair, and says, *Fine. Very fine.*
You swim with buffalo in the river. A child
washes her mother there. She pulls off a piece

of the dead woman's shoulder and shares it
with her father.

You are wearing white robes when I see you.
I finger a gift of Himalayan fossils
and cannot name one bone. This was my home too,
now every room smells of woodsmoke. Rags blessed
by the Dalai Lama hang at the windows, yellow muslin
and ink fading as they fly prayers
onto a humid East River night.

In Nepal, you tell me, love is easy,
all wheels are spun clockwise, and the dead
are buried comfortably in the walls
of their own homes.

SUSAN TICHY

The Bus from Sagada:
Passing a Sacred Mountain

Philippines

The man is trying to talk the boy
into giving me a flower. The boy
has been eating his flowers,
petal by petal, rolling each one
between his palms, then peeling away
the long yellow fibers, placing
the sweet pink between his lips.
Now he puts his shoes on the seat in front
and grins his small embarrassment.
I am large and single, like a calla.
He is just one of the Everlasting.
But the man is still prodding his shoulder—
he won't stop. So the boy,

though he's only seven or eight,
sits up straight with his hands on his knees:
there is something he has to do.

This flower has been carried from the boy's home.
Perhaps it was given to him.
Perhaps he pulled it
from a neighbor's bush as he passed.
It's damp, when he hands it to me, and cool.
One petal has been torn away
and a drop of nectar dangles at the wound.
The man is talking a mile a minute,
and laughing. The boy is shy.
And I don't know if I'm expected
to eat the flower too.
I decide not. Steam

is beginning to rise from the carrots
and cauliflower packed in over the engine.
The night guard, on his way back to town,
sits dozing over his rifle. He too is damp,
and just a boy, with red wool socks
pulled over the legs of his trousers.
Pulag says the man with the grin, and points
to one dark side
of the mountain I had forgotten.

Everlasting is the name given to wreaths and leis of dried flowers, seen everywhere in the cordillera of Northern Luzon.

"From now on . . ."

From now on I am a road
just reaching the top of a hill—
I go on but I can't see where.

Let rain fall. Let breath
condense on the dirty glass.
The present is my house

and my house is full of children.
I lift each one above my head, and shake out
the armies that fly from their mouths.

Some of the children speak plainly.
Some comb out their tangled hair.
Some pack the suitcase
they'll carry to the next life.

But what I love and what I hate—
I'm letting go of their hands,
those two poor twins.
Who will take them in?

The sun will shrivel, the rain distend,
and the wind will roll me over in her arms.
No one will know what size shoes
I was wearing, not even me.

It will be "the day of labor,
the night of gunfire" forever.
No decisions but the necessary ones.
And no more nights like this one.

From now on I am a road of stone,
hewn, and mortared to the hill.
When a man strikes his foot against my shoulder
let him swear, let him stoop to rub the bruise,

and rest where a cypress blocks the wind
like a shawled woman turning her back.

At a Cock Fight

Philippines

As special guests we're seated
on stools in the crowd of men.
The chanting—that stopped
when we entered, their bodies
pressed back in two stunned waves—

44

begins again, a drum
of two hundred voices, beaten
by the raised, waving fist
of the *soltador*. The bets
take time to collect. The birds
don't want to fight, are urged.
We're told they don't feel pain
as we do, just instinct old as dirt.
This too takes time.
There's a bird in the arms
of a young boy standing near us
that doesn't fight. It's there
to rile the rest:
they hold the fighting bird
and let the other peck it
till it bleeds. Released, the cock
sees only one opponent: it's beautiful
when the feathers on its neck stand up—
gold, black, green, red. The men
stand perfectly still, tense
under their old, loose-fitting clothes.
The only sound is the proud,
random crowing of cocks who wait their turn.
You hear the touch of claw on dust, as the birds
circle with lowered heads . . . They leap
face-high, hanging
on carefully trimmed wings, slash
down the green, the white, the red . . .
then land, stare blankly
at each other. The *soltador*
prods them, holds one while the other
pecks its face. They can't understand
the razors, why a simple nasty temper
smells like death. One's lost
coordination, falls on its chin.
The other pounces, pecks its eyes,
looks round at the human noise.
But neither has died. He picks them up
by the scruff of the neck
and shakes them. Sometimes

45

there's a clear winner. Sometimes
when he drops them both fall down.
Blood and feathers
stick to his arms. His concentration
is marvelous, as the shouts
go an octave higher, everyone
pressing forward, jumping, and waving
their fists in the air, except us. We sit
on our plastic stools, engulfed
by their bodies, see nothing. *Nothing*
will happen to you. We have twenty boys
strung out between here and the road.
I told the head man, Don't
let this place get raided
with two Americans here.
Sweat runs from a clenched fist
over a stringy back, soaks into a pair of old blue pants:
that's all we know.
It's over when the crowd
breaks up in a brawl over money.
The loser is one
of the ones who can't feel pain.
It pushes itself through the dirt
with legs that don't work, aren't
connected anymore to its brain. No one
is watching the rapt expression
on the face of the man who sheathes
the razors, kicks dust over the blood.

The *soltador* is the handler of cocks in the fighting pit.

JOY HARJO

Resurrection

Estelí
      this mountain town means something
                  like the glass of bloody stars.
Your Spanish tongue will not be silent.
                          In my volcano heart,
soldiers pace, watch over what they fear.
          One pretty one leans against his girlfriend
they make promises, touch, plan to meet somewhere else
                        in this war.
Not far down the fevered street
             a trace of calypso
                laughter from a cantina.
We are all in a balloon that's about to split.
               Candles make oblique circles
in the barrio church, line the walls with prayers.
                An aboriginal woman
as old as Momotombo fingers obsidian
             recalls dreams, waits for the light
to begin to break. I don't imagine anything.
             Lizards chase themselves all night
over the tin roof of the motel.
                I rock in a barrage of fever,
feel the breathing-sweat of the whole town: stop, pause
                   and begin again.
I have no damned words to make violence fit neatly
               like wrapped packages
of meat, to hold us safely.
         The songs here speak tenderly of honor and love,
sweet melody is the undercurrent of gunfire,
                    yet
the wounded and the dead call out in words that sting
             like bitter limes. Ask the women
who have given away the clothes of their dead children.
Ask the frozen soul of a man who was found buried in

47

the hole left by his missing penis.
They are talking, yet
                    the night could change.
We all watch for fire
                    for all the fallen dead to return
and teach us a language so terrible
                            it could resurrect us all.

Nine Below

Across the frozen Bering Sea is the invisible border
of two warring countries. I am loyal to neither,

only to the birds who fly over, laugh at the ridiculous
ways of humans, know wars destroy dreams, divide the

country, inside us. Last night there was a breaking
wave, in the center of a dream war. You were there, but

I couldn't see you. Woke up cold in a hot house. Didn't
sleep but fought the distances I had imagined, and went

back to find you. I called my heart's dogs, gave them
the sound of your blue saxophone to know you by, and let

them smell the shirt you wore when we last made love.
I walked with them south along the white sea, and

crossed to the fiery plane of my dreaming. We circled
the place; you weren't there. I found nothing I could see,

no trace of war, of you, but the dogs barked, rolled
in your smell, ears pricked at what they could hear that

I couldn't. They ran to me, licked the smell of the wet
tracks of your mouth from my neck, my shoulder. They

smelled your come on my fingers, my face. They felt the
quivering nerve of emotion that forced me to live. It

made them nervous excited. I loosened my mind's rein;
let them find you.

I watched them follow the invisible connection. They
traveled a spiral arc through an Asiatic burst of time.

There were no false boundaries between countries, between
us. They climbed the polar ice, saw it melt.

They flew through the shimmering houses of the gods,
crossed over into your childhood, and then south.

When they arrived in your heart's atmosphere it was
an easy sixty degrees. The war was over, it had never

begun, and you were alive and laughing, standing beneath
a fat sun, calling me home.

STEVEN WHITE

Abandoned at 4,000 Meters

A sudden jolt and everything stops.
We're on the border
of madness. All the zeros
on this money from Bolivia
make me nervous,
make my backpack heavier.

It is night but no one sleeps
on our decapitated train
dead on the tracks
of a single desert
divided into two countries.

I see the engine
chug toward the stars
leaving its body behind.

And my poor pounding head!

Workers in dirty overalls
come from nowhere
with tools

and too much time.
They begin to crawl beneath us.

Speculators wonder if their bones
will be checked for contraband.
They would even invest in this darkness
for the tiniest of profits.

I shiver by a window
that is useless because here
the wind blows through glass.

Crossing the Plain of Patience

The return from our past was always painful.
Because it wasn't as if we had regained life,
but that we had lost it once again
in the earth covered with what grows.
We found ourselves
thinking of the barren place,
remembering how we could cross
the plain of patience
and navigate dunes in fierce winds
below a sun that watched us like an open wound.

Here was the paradise we could seek forever.
Only our particles dispersed like light.
Only the alternate deserts of our lives.
Only the absence of desire.

Where we left our dreams
and flooded our fields
and measured each syllable of water,
was the edge of the oasis.
Then we would step into desolation
and a stronger vision:
the night so clear
we could hear the stars
and the dead who had slept like babies
in their womb of sand
as they soared over the great necropolis.

The desert rocks were our eyes—
bare, beyond moisture, ductless.
It made no sense to weep
for trees that never were.

There was no longing for the life
that shriveled and blew through immensity
or for all the lives that disappeared
in the void of history.

For the desert was the emptiness that grew
within us and, here, our prayers
rose without fear from a handful of dust.
Everything we could have known
knelt before us
as if we were greater than what we knew.

NANCY MAIRS

To Virginia (and Points West)

1

"how the dead sing behind rhododendron bushes"

> V.W., *Mrs. Dalloway*

> *Everything, in time,*
> *takes very long.*

The press of white lawn
against white stocking, the curve
of breast, shoulder, the stiff feathers
of the birdie shot from the raquet
—thwack!—dove-white against the sky!

He lies on his back in the grass

under the elm, blazer open,
one arm thrown across his eyes.

> *None of this,*
> *I promise you, is true.*

Under the bridge the fish hang
in the water, slips of silver, heads
turned upstream. He leans out,
imagining himself a fish, the brown water
against his flanks. He feeds on minnows.

She leans further, imagining herself
Ophelia, turning slowly in the pinnace
of her white garments downstream,
scattering dead-men's-fingers, dirty songs.

> *There is a miracle.*
> *It is no longer fashionable*
> *to name it.*
> *It was called love.*

She waits in the shadows
for the first touch. Her skin is whiter
than the dress at her feet.
When his fingers stroke her breasts
they tremble and swing like mute bells.

> *Not until death do we*
> *enter an eternity of song.*

2

"we know not why we go upstairs, or why we come down
     again"

V.W., *Orlando*

In the morning
I rescue a toad from a pool of brown water
and put him under the squash leaves.

Later I find him
halfway engorged by a striped
garter snake.

Excusing myself,
I twist three furry zucchinis
from their stalks, carry them
into the kitchen for supper.

Now I hear
someone knocking at the front door.
If I answered, I could ask:
Why have you come here?

A light mist pearls
above the alfalfa field. The drops
on the nacreous flesh of the cut zucchinis
wet my fingers, the knife.

Light fails. The dragons
have fallen asleep
at the bottom of the garden.

3

"But still—I eat up the black and doubtful pieces of meat
   in memory—"

V.W., *Letters*

Fixed,

a retinal burn in time:

On dry pine needles, the sky
pewter through the thinning trees,
she tries to spread her legs
shackled by terror.

The scene enacts, reenacts
itself (the butting cock, the knees
arthritic with fear). No matter:

that she dreams of orgasm
in the arms of a giant
the color of clay, whimpers once,
wakes with eyes empty as the sky;

that he
has gone to West Virginia again
to think.

4

"others are hundreds of years old though they call
    themselves thirty-six."

V.W., *Orlando*

Next week
at the dark of the moon
I turn thirty-six.

The bats will swoop,
chittering, from the barns, the trees,
and cover my eyes
tight with their leathery wings.

From the tall grass
the fox will come up,
parting the blades with his sharp nose,
and bite my throat.

I will turn and turn
forever blind and dumb in the tug
of earth under the absence of moon.

4

"I am old; I am ugly. I am repeating things."

V.W., *A Writer's Diary*

In the dusk bats drop
and flitter over a theatre of grass.

There are fireflies
among the burning poppies.

No hand touches my chill skin
except in dreams.

I might
have lived another life.

JIMMY SANTIAGO BACA

XI.

Adobe brick.
Mix sand and water as mortar.
Palm it on, lay the adobe down,
smooth out the overlapping mud,
then let it dry.
The simplicity of this type of building,
becomes music,
a heavy melody of whispers of my hands
in mud, my fingers hushing,
until slowly the mud dries and my fingers scratch-rub
out designs, niches for santos,
horno to keep pan warm—
I stand back after days of work
to appraise my sculptured figure—
like Rilke in front of a Grecian statue—
I live inside this one,
part of its blood-mud, I move slowly
inside its body like a dream.
A man will cook in here, sleep in here,
will stare outside into the world
at others staring inside.
Life inside of life—
closed bud waits until its time
to blossom—and who can envision
    the soft-sparkle of beauty
in the blossom,
before the eye and heart sees it?
Who knows what poems will come
    from this little adobe casita?
Who lingers inside this adobe casita?
What will I blossom into?
Like a seed, I crouch in my work,
nestled in this carved and dried earth.
The drowsy sleep that absorbs

the dormant fields this time of year,
absorbs me—
I am creating myself in this mud and adobe.
The sun, when I walk outside,
buzzes down on me like a honey bee,
taking some sweetness from me,
then in a huffy swirl, buzzes across the fields,
through the bare elm branches.
And as I hose myself off,
hose off the spatters of mud from my face and arms,
I see in my head
a newborn child being washed off by a midwife,
its blood is toweled off,
a warm wash cloth is applied to its small body,
as I let water run down my arms.

JOSEPH HUTCHISON

Thunderhead

A tall cloud sleepwalks
out of mountains. Its weight
—the memory of
a drowned child—bows
down my head . . . as when
a plunging elevator
suddenly slows:
held breath; the heart-valve
struggle of the doors. Already

the storm's an abandoned
steeple, father-shaped, bell
a coyote's muzzle blurred
by a shower curtain. Underfoot,
my toes feel the grass

56

of a bathmat weave
and unweave the light
of my feelings, the oblique
shadow-light. Far off, I know

the child's kneeling again
by the flood stream. His milky
face on the swirls seems
weightless,
a cloud. As always, he
bends to touch it: how motherly
and dark my current's pull!
I gaze up at him
and smile. But when his arms
embrace me, the old panic
breaks their hold

and the dream river
turns to a ditch
of red mud, down which the howls
that wake me vanish
like thunder.

Walking Off a Night of Drinking in Early Spring

for Joe Nigg

Through the budding elm branches, eyes
of traffic lights blink red to green;
the idled traffic surges forward in the dark—

and we stagger on down the alley, joyful,
voices loud and cloudy in the cold.
Where do these hours come from? Hours

when old wounds flare, and the night
opens, and pain boils up into conversation,
as if talk can heal. The sweating bottle

drifts hand to hand, mouth to mouth—
and stars blink through branching clouds,
the blood groping darkly in our heads;

but the moon's here, too. A bright clarity
over cars and streetlamps, over houses
and leaving trees: going with us.

PAUL HUNTER

Dear Reader

Sometimes you want out and
sometimes I want to oblige you
like a hitchhiker gone sour
who's got his boots parked
on my dash and when I point
kicks 'em both off and
cocks up his smelly feet

who keeps asking what there is to eat
and never offers his hidden pint
who says huh to everything I say
like I'm lying through my teeth
who swats at the crow feather
garter on my mirror and says
that the kinda animals you like?

And as the wheels bite
the gravel shoulder and waver
I finger the tire iron
with no room to swing it
and think of rolling us
into the drainage ditch
for the muddy hell of it

and slam to a halt and say
well this is it for ya
you plead hey make it the turnoff
the next town this is no way to be
stuck in the hot sun
no one in his right mind stops
in a cornfield the middle of nowhere

I say you shoulda thought a that
and watch you unlimber
and take your sweet old time
considering the car full of junk
and this skinny guy with the big
knuckles and bloodshot eyes
that could go off any minute.

A Sinking No a Rising
No a Sinking Feeling

All wood that falls to water
migrates toward the emptiness.

Some waterlog early and decay,
look at yourself
sunk to the chin, look, look!
You did not enter
the salt water that way.

If you had not accepted
it as your element
drained your sap and opened
every pore to drink
deep of the life beyond you

that seems to lift but engulfs
the you that is never satisfied

if it were not for the desire
of the tree to walk upon water

the thirst of the boat to be fish
you would still float high and empty

Goodbye to Marian

A friend is dying I
hesitate to go visit.
What is it I fear?
A stain on these white sheets,
a sudden shrinking of you
to nothing as I watch?

I already treasure
you as you once were.
Even miraculous cures
could not make you over.
I would not have you otherwise.

And I tell myself I am fragile.
Why risk being derailed
just as my life is
rolling nicely?

But is this still a slight rise
or long level, or
the inevitable downhill slide?

Cezanne would not give up
a day's painting to
bury his own mother.
And my own mother dying
could not hand me her goodbye.

So are the living heartless?
Or is the counsel
of death not always wise?

With a little shame
I write a love note
and at a distance release you.
I am not all that strong, I admit it.

Going down you may take
my hand and with one look
draw and draw and draw me.

DAVID CHORLTON

Ainadamar

on the death of Garcia Lorca

Broken glass falls out of Federico's eyes.
In the grey light
his other dawns are washed
in the fountain, fountain of stars,
fountain that weeps

with the black wives
who look for their husbands in hands
rising from the bones.
Ainadamar,

fountain named for sorrow
long before Federico
drew a lizard in the air
when he felt a cold shadow
cross his back on the train, train
to his city which sings

in its caves.
Ainadamar, water
through the Arabic night,
through sand to the jasmine

that keeps Granada awake.
The night climbs all Granada's stairs,
knocks on its doors

and knows nothing.
Dark heels count the men
who sleepwalk from their doors

and are gone before the birds
reclaim their songs
and the cherry trees bleed.
Night of black coffee,

Federico touches clean linen
from home and unfolds
doves in the steam from his broth,

flying in the smoke
of another last cigarette. Sweet tobacco,
chicken broth and the ice
on a guard's face.

Behind the cemetery wall, the deaf
hear the dawn
punch holes in voiceless bricks.
The cypress does not hide them.
The prayers do not fill them.
Ainadamar

flows to the Albaicin
where dark faces turn
into ash. Beyond the olive groves

Federico sweats black water
as the sun spits
long rays across the leaves
and ties the hands of the clock.
As Federico sings

his voice wraps the bullet,
he swallows the seed
of the olive and his lungs turn to oil.
Ainadamar, deaf stream

from the petals closing
on Federico's lips as it mourns
his blood to the bright geraniums
in the Albaicin, Ainadamar,
the red kiss, the bitter spring.

The Mormon Chronicler

William Clayton is counting fractions
of a mile from the Mississippi
to the Great Salt Lake. He walks

beside a wagon wheel
on which a cloth is tied
to mark each revolution. Clayton whispers

numbers like a prayer
along the road to Zion. He describes
the streams and dust, the depth

of soil and water
and the distance from one camp to the next,
writing as he goes

directions to a valley blessed
and waiting. His eyes are fixed
on the terrain

as a new sun arcs
above the train. The edges of America
turn from grass to rock

and the sky lifts
with the miles until
the space between the earth and heaven

is enough for a new religion.
The red cloth keeps rising at Clayton's shoulder.
He is faithful

to every detail of the trail.
As he records the journey
he threads a rosary of stones.

HAROLD LITTLEBIRD

Blue Lake Journey

grey dripping clouds
blanket Taos peak in thin layers of swirling rain
more piled high, move swiftly
block dull morning sun

pack, repack
enough food for weeks and only five people
those not going feel sorry for our horses

tighten ropes against saddles
one last check
everyone wishes us "safe journey"
bids us be careful
turns colder each minute

through narrow wooden gate
along mud-pooled road
eastward toward beckoning mountains
follow sloppy trails across corn stubble fields
upward, gradual ascent
pause, break out ponchos
amid juniper foothills and pinon

against melodic plodding of hoofbeats
settle into hard saddles
ford a muddy river twice
angling away from graded road
joining rougher, single-filed slippery trail
everyone excited, joking
full of good cheer
we begin steep climb
under sheer wall of silent rain

near midday, break through shroudlike fog
drizzle falls steadily in misty sheets
ascend drenched mountain

shiver beneath rain slick ponchos
horses' steadfast pace echoes like a round dance song
far down hidden canyons

fog lifts
we wear ceaseless rain like outer layer of wet clothing
pause to tighten loose cinches, adjust and shift saddle bags
balance bulky weight

finally stop for first night
in a clearing beneath towering spruce
peer west in falling light
across far and murky horizon
grey sagebrush flats, obscure tiny peaks
little bumps that interrupt a barren plain

morning comes enveloped in dense fog
moist cover dampens saddles and gear
we leave our spruce tree camp
climb higher
air much colder
trail quite slippery from all night rain
cautiously, our horses pick their way
shake off morning chill
a welcome sun breaks through rolling layered clouds
hinting of snow

enter treeless sunlit meadow
patches of azure appear
between racing winter clouds
and a bitter swirling wind
catches us in the open
but we are very near I am told
just beyond snow packed pass and down a farther canyon

topping pass, shivering from head to toe
we dismount one last time
out of nowhere, large golden eagle shrieks, greets us
rides uplift currents, glides rim
disappears behind distant rocky ridge

step carefully to jutted overhang
of wind smooth rock

squint through biting wind
gaze upon that place of strength and prayer
for first time
far below, tranquil, undisturbed on a narrow point
shimmering beneath steep cliff face
a powerful turquoise gem
serene against darkened sky
my heart pauses respectfully, full of wonder

zig-zag burdened horses gingerly
down gently sloping trail
brilliant knee high flowers
lavender, lemon, red encircle us, dip graceful petals
suddenly transform into swaying, breathing rainbow

near clean, clear creek trickling into old beaver pond
we hurriedly unpack wet gear
stash everything we won't need beneath plastic tarps
tie exhausted horses amidst long summer grass
to fill their hungry bellies
with numb hands and soggy wood
struggle to build small fire
for hot chocolate and coffee
chilling rain turns to sleet, to heavy snow
we crawl wearily inside make-shift tent

September 12th, summer gone
peek out on icy winter world
leaky tarp begins to sag, drip from wet snow
night swallows secluded camp
eyes heavy, tucked warmly inside down bag
snoring of companions fills cold, placid air
I look forward to a night's rest
but that solemn vision looms clearly in my mind
on snow capped summit, my eyes beheld momentarily
the power, the magic

SCOTT DAVIDSON

The Colossus

after Francisco Goya

Our descent out of oak and red willow ends
where the river stalls, turning on itself,
and this valley concedes its horizon.
South, the twin arcs of the cooling tower break
into concrete bloom, leaving an edge
of light where they meet the air,
like oil and water refusing to blend.
Under our wheels the interstate veers.

In the *Dream of Reason,* a studious man
sleeps face down in his book. Bats swarm
like flies overhead, thicker as the light
of the spent candle fades. This removed,
he will never wake in time to see the bats
transform, watch them pour from his window,
darkening the moon like a factory cloud.
Beyond the reach of domestic lights,

the Colossus juts above talus and weeds,
thunderheads forming like threats at his back.
Eyes etched unconscious as rocks, he turns
his glare on shacks near the ground, scans the valley
without recognition, reduces the town
to incidental walls. He remembers no ties
to these people or their land. He is free
to level anything in his way.

Fifty miles from Oklahoma, the cooling tower broods.
Four lanes of interstate keep backing down.
Stalled near the river, my wife and I watch
from behind tempered glass. We make our home
in the stucco town. We are accidents of blood,
villagers who recognize ominous signs and didn't

67

say a word. The man on the news spoke our shred
of perfect trust. He said, *everyone has a job.*

Once the tower's behind us, the interstate runs.
Drinking coffee in a truck stop, we don't let on
to these locals what we know, how this morning
the Air Force lost a warhead near Damascus, how they
emptied the town and still played dumb. Bats give way
to threat and storm. The studious man finally wakes,
watches clouds swarm at his window convinced
no one could have known and no one can be blamed.

Approaching Equinox

See it on my hands,
where the rake handle blistered my palms,
the infrared glow of my skin
reflecting the light of a three-way bulb,
or stand on my porch and smell
autumn like a spice in the air.

Each day the sun clings
hand over hand to the sky, and each day it drowns
further along the horizon, closer to the stand
of cedar that marks the day sunlight loses
its edge, and darkness is a tide
inching its way up the beach.

Tonight I stop what I'm doing and watch
the pull of earth turn the sky to glass,
the sun's hands scrape their defiance
of gravity. Tonight I choose to sink
with the light. The heat of my body
leaks through my shoes, my bones fill with air

and I'm hollowed like a gourd for drumming,
my skin the surface of a tambourine
in constant, delicious vibration. My porch is the hub
to a wheel of stars. When I give in to this last
long summer day, I'm the echo of breathing,
the tangible history of wind.

BARBARA LA MORTICELLA

Truths (An Oral Poem)

A distant galaxy spins like a pinwheel.
Its arms are radio signals with two tones
coming to us from across all of space:

EEEEEEEEEEEEEEEE   OOOOOOOOOOOOOOOOO

The bushmen in the Kalahari say that they
can hear the stars, for they are noisy.

They say there are worlds out there
so far away we cannot see them . . .

sun, moons, and people like us,
planets that are being born and dying.

They say there are three worlds:
the first is the earth,
the second, the realm of the gods of the earth,
the third, of the thousands of planets.

But they say the third world is of no concern:
what's important to us is life on earth,
what makes life on earth possible.

2.

The Zulus say we can't know the ultimate truth.
The best we can do is tell stories that describe the truth,
but these stories will change as we change.
In the overall scheme of things, the earth is no more
than an insect's playball rolled in the dust.

This depresses white culture,
which doesn't do well with subtleties.
It wants to find evidence of life in space,
if it has to pave over the continents as a launching pad.
It's all or nothing:
If the earth isn't the center of the universe,
it's a ball of dung.

But I think that rocket ships are the wrong way
to travel:

There's a patch of violet that lives behind my right eye
that I know comes from the third world,
and it just won't stop singing.

Horsetail Rush

All winter
the horsetails
have been lying under
                     the ground,

polishing their heads
and doing   shrinking
            exercises.

Armed only with the
tiny blades of cells,
they rush through asphalt
at the sun's knock
                  on the stone.

Ancient tribe
that knows the wisdom
                  underneath
our roads:

Pebbles roll
like prayer shawls
around the females
as they
            emerge,
stout as clubs,
phallic and
            fertile;

while the males spin,
frothy and

                frilly,
    though they are
                bristling.

PATRICIA DUBRAVA

April Icon

Jumbled femurs and ribs
lie along Piney Creek,
the remains of scavenging.
The printmaker found this morkin,
came grinning home with it,
the souvenir skull still noble,
jawbone fitting beneath
like a puzzle's easy, final piece.

Natives say it's good luck
to find the skeleton of a horse,
better by far than the narrow bones
of sheep, or the broad heads of cows.
Every cattle guard gateway
has its decorations of those,
raised for slaughter and so less prized.
The horse is another matter:
semi-retired servant,
seat of romantic re-enactments.
The printmaker packed his winter kill
keepsake in a California van, drove away.

Wind gushes through cottonwoods
like a waterfall, and Piney Creek
gurgles over smooth stones.
Large chalky bones are twigs
in the hand.

(The April 1984 blizzard:
the horse floundering in drifts
to his barrel chest, going down,
legs folding into white.)

These porous relics are light
and dry as pipe dreams.
The printmaker imagines he's taken
fortune with him,
but luck left its body here,
rose like incense in clear Wyoming air.

What It's Like in Wyoming

The meadow lark sings in fenced pastures.
In the creek, three large brown trout
hold against the current, contemplating.
When a shadow touches the bank,
they double and disappear.
Mule deer scatter among cottonwoods,
ford the confluence of creeks
in three easy leaps,
gray coats melting into sage.

A truck's changing gears carry
half a mile from the time it rounds
the mesa till it hits the fork
past the bridge.
The meadow lark stitches silence
back together under a sky heavy
with hope of rain.

Stone-ringed memories of encampment
fade on a high hilltop.
One could raise the rubbed hide flap
of a teepee, look down
to box elder-fringed water,
up to the Big Horns, slate blue and white.
One would see the valley without fences,

72

that ranch house gone,
the occasional whisper of tires gone,
that golden eagle climbing a spiral
in primordial air.
It would be like that.
It is like that sometimes still.

KARL KOPP

The Greater Sun

> *"Local woman sees image of Christ in breakfast dough.*
> *Church says not a miracle. . . ."*

The green stucco home   neat and clean
its windows sparkling   houses a "shrine"

   the portico of magic and of mystery

for a flour tortilla with a striking pattern
of skillet burn marks which hundreds and perhaps
thousands of people believe is a likeness of Jesus
the Christ

She sees the pattern
and we make of it mountain-ranges and castles
galleons and continents   slow silent horses   water
and air to form   doodlings of God   stigmata
in the white dogwood streaked with rose

Her ancestors saw a greater sun   his face their own
who wears our daily sun on a necklace

   "What it will be Questioned   When the Sun rises
   do you not see a round Disk of fire somewhat
   like a Guinea O no no I see an Innumerable

73

company of the Heavenly Host crying Holy
Holy Holy is the Lord God Almighty"

I was rolling my husband's burrito
and on the first roll I noticed something
which looked like a face   I just stood there
not moving because it looked like the face of Jesus

"Stand still and see the salvation of the Lord"

And this from years of ikons   holy paintings
stained-glass windows of the mind?

We are more than we think we see   she sees
as Malinche the god in the uncouth Spaniard saw
son of the sun   she sees as Blake and as blind Milton saw

It looked like the face of Jesus   the wing
in the egg   the spring in the sun—
baked ground

I just stood there   not moving
the pattern past our gods and lovers
because it looked like the face of Jesus

she sees through centuries of slow
silent meditations   our heart's
own desire in the daily
oracle of bread

Ahead the Pacific

Ahead the Pacific   cold at dusk
our trees bent double in the wind from Asia
bent double like ancient crones   a world apart
a world of water and stars

But the lights   those lights across the lot beckon
to bodies   to young bodies at the bar   to waitresses
to food and money

                        And travelers we face
the wind   struggle for direction
and breath

> Two large dogs   two mastiffs face the sea
in the bed of their master's truck   the wind
carves their dark fur back
outlining   as in stone

> those ishii on temple gates guard
emptiness   observe a something other
at dusk   in the setting sun

not watching us as we fight by   not guarding
our world   not seeing what we see

GRETEL EHRLICH

A Hawk's Winter Landing

You call me one night and say,
"Better come on up here and keep me warm."
So I drive to the ranch.
Everywhere the white refrains of winter
carol out and out ahead of me.
Snowdrifts roll up and fall back from
the pickup until your house appears,
one planet of light
in this
Arctic sea.

At the door, you hold me.
It's like being gathered into
a nest of wishbones
all breaking in my favor.
"I love those mountains," you say,
the brim-sweat on your hat standing
in a halo of peaks around your head.
As I look at your face, your eyes
sew with tropical stitches
everything stark in me.

75

"It's a hard camp here," you warn me,
"Pipes froze, no heat,
nothing fancy in the way of food."
We go to a room.
As we undress, I dowse you
with haydust from morning,
those bright clippings scribbled fast
across your back as if to spell out
the emergency of being together,
the restraint we feel.

You get into bed
with your boots on.
I ask why. "Gal," you say,
"If I take them off,
I'll fall in love with you."
A draft in the room
roams us as if we belonged
to its spell, drifting and
banking over our two lives,
awkward on the swayback bed.

"Sweetheart," you say. "All these years . . ."
Outside snow begins to fall.
". . . I've wanted you . . ."
It falls and is gathered in a willow's hairnet of frailty.
". . . And now I'm afraid once I start . . ."
It spills on itself and sifts double.
". . . I won't be able to stop . . ."
Against the house, trees rattling.
". . . I'd like nothing better
than to die in your arms this way. . . ."

All night the drifts pull fans of white marriage rice
across us as if snow were beads of desire hurrying
to close the road. I say,
"If we are people on whom nothing is lost,
it only matters that we do not lose the night and who we are."
    You turn to me. Even at forty, you're scared.
My hands go to your boots. I pull at the heels.
Your feet fly free. Your whole body floats up

like a hawk who might be lifting
out of a tree but is really landing.

Probably She Is A River

Probably she is a river where
seasonal mixtures run
rich: watercress, hot springs, ice floes stacked
in clerical collars on robes of
dark water folding and
unfolding around her.

Probably she lost track
of her reflection in the armed ambush
of willow stands.
She will not say her name.

Here is where
all the collisions of storms
fall out and swim home.

She rides those
hard boxcars with other
hoboes of winter: snowdrift, comet tail,
wounded deer.

Here, at the rapids,
she navigates her thin hips into surrenders.
Those strangers hunt and
touch and drink her longing to be invisible.

They do not fatten on it.

She loves them so she wants
to be their one predator.
They love her so they want her
wildness to be hunted in them.

They tow her on
thin train-floats of driftwood
into warm spots and out again past
bullet holes of rocks.

All her waters and liquors pulled this way.

Probably she cries out.
"I'm sinking."
Despite this vanity,
the river opens and accepts.

She is the water that carries her.

JOHN BRADLEY

Moonrise: Hernandez, New Mexico, 1941

What good is a corpse, if it is not named
Juan, or Jacinta, or Cuerpo del Hombre?
What good is a knucklebone, if you can't roll it
gambling with infinity for the moon?
Why this Spanish fluttering through my ribs?
What good is invisibility if I can't darken
the sky over Hernandez with the turn of my wrist?

Look into my eyes and you will see
the dark eyes of that Apache woman, she
who died when they cut the cord
that held us, me to her. She floats
when I look into the waterbarrel
like a window in a mountain lake.
A radio barks an ad for soap, or soup.
I don't know who got her pregnant.
The one, maybe, who cut the cord
with his dull knife.

Come with us, Miguelito, the wind calls to me.
For a few centavos of a minute, come.
The starlight on the shoulders of the sage
that's who your father is.

Come into the black bean where night hides
from the four deaths of the day.
Well, Miguel, shall we go?
But he never answers.

Love, that's the opening in your side
the knife leaves, and all the faces rush out.
Those who have only their hunger, those who hurt,
those who want you to lie down and hold them.
Sometimes, I do. This makes them not better,
just not as sad, for a while.
The Apache woman, she doesn't know why
she is sad, only that she wants me to nurse
on her thin, funeral water.

What good is a man if all he can do is rake
the gravel up over his chest?
What good is the wind, sin carne like that
when it can't lick you clean with its smooth claws?

So This is the World: Biloxi, 1943

The spiteful laziness of the lazy
Salamander, its tongue melting

The mountain in a drop of water.
So this is the world. The accusing

Eyes of the owl Daddy stuffed.
It bothers me, knowing

Each day is the last, each day.
Sex, Daddy said, is vital, but

It's Tuesday, I'm out of mayonnaise.
Something's always leaving me.

The salamander's fishy flesh
Behind the druggist's ear.

He rubbed my nipples. I read
The WARNING on my prescription.

Is it raining? the clock asks.
Even, sometimes, when it's raining.

The screen door, I love the anger
Of the flies, holds itself

Shut. Go ahead, bore your way
Into my heart. Tell me

You can't get enough.

TED KOOSER

In The Basement of the Goodwill Store

In musty light, in the thin brown air
of damp carpet, doll heads and rust,
beneath long rows of sharp footfalls
like nails in a lid, an old man stands
trying on glasses, lifting each pair
from the box like a glittering fish
and holding it up to the light
of a dirty bulb. Near him, a heap
of enameled pans as white as skulls
looms in the catacomb shadows,
and old toilets with dry red throats
cough up bouquets of curtain rods.

You've seen him somewhere before.
He's wearing the green leisure suit
you threw out with the garbage,
and the Christmas tie you hated,
and the ventilated wingtip shoes
you found in your father's closet
and wore as a joke. And the glasses
which finally fit him, through which

80

he looks to see you looking back—
two mirrors which flash and glance—
and those through which one day
you too will look down over the years,
when you have grown old and thin
and no longer particular,
and the things you once thought
you were rid of forever
have taken you back in their arms.

Abandoned Farmhouse

He was a big man, says the size of his shoes
on a pile of broken dishes by the house;
a tall man too, says the length of the bed
in an upstairs room; and a good, God-fearing man,
says the Bible with a broken back
on the floor below the window, dusty with sun;
but not a man for farming, say the fields
cluttered with boulders and the leaky barn.

A woman lived with him, says the bedroom wall
papered with lilacs and the kitchen shelves
covered with oilcloth, and they had a child,
says the sandbox made from a tractor tire.
Money was scarce, say the jars of plum preserves
and canned tomatoes sealed in the cellar hole.
And the winters cold, say the rags in the window frames.
It was lonely here, says the narrow country road.

Something went wrong, says the empty house
in the weed-choked yard. Stones in the fields
say he was not a farmer; the still-sealed jars
in the cellar say she left in a nervous haste.
And the child? Its toys are strewn in the yard
like branches after a storm—a rubber cow,
a rusty tractor with a broken plow,
a doll in overalls. Something went wrong, they say.

81

Geronimo's Mirror

That flash from a distant hillside,
that firefly in the blue shadows of rock—
that's Geronimo's mirror.
After all of these years, he's up there
still trying to warn us
that the soldiers are coming.
He sees them riding along the horizon
in an endless line,
sees them dipping down into the valley
rider by rider.
His mirror or tin, cupped in his palm,
says they're nearer now.
It says he can hear the black rock
sounding under their hooves,
can smell the sharp smoke of dust in the air.
Now he can hear their dark voices,
the old voices of horses,
and the talk that is leather's.
And now they are climbing the hill,
that holy hill that is Geronimo's,
but he is not afraid.
His mirror is warning the others,
and we are the others.

CHRISTOPHER HOWELL

We Who Have Found Wisdom

We who have found wisdom
address you
who have not. We think, "Holy Cow!"
and "Salutations!" The water near us is
certainly full of itself. And the air is misty

with the imported electricity of our perceptions.
Oh there are the geese, flying east
for some reason. The ferries
are on time. Nothing changes, except now
that we know it, the secret key
that causes life to mean
and not mean everything, what can be
sucked from the odd moment? What can you give us
whose wisdom is like a crowd
of ravenous and hostile pockets devouring their trousers?
But that's all right, all right; we're wise,
compensated and alone here
and there and, though we of course already know,
   we are just calling
and calling to ask how you are.

The Cry

The moon hangs in alders
by the bridge. Something is crying out
down there in the choked hollow,
down there in the grass. Trapped
or maybe bereft, it trumpets
up the ladders of mist and cold
as if nothing mattered anymore
except voice hefting the exact fullness
of this moment in which something
is terribly wrong.

I am afraid of you,
whatever you are, and of your grief
or pain sung like a gift
that no one wants. Once, I think,
I will come down to you
through scotch broom and heaps of leaves
and put my fingers softly
to your throat and stroke you and feel
the dense shiver of language
leaving you, seeking my nameless body

somewhere outside of what we are
in daylight or in summer.

But it's autumn now and I don't want to die
or hear you, dying fascination. I don't
want the frayed rim of your call
looking back to me out of my hands
and scuffling shoes. Yet you cannot
be still and the long word rasps
again onto the air.

An owl calls a few times: testing
testing. I turn toward home,
nudging aside pity, guilt, and echoes
of the suffering every creature knows.
Nothing changes what I cannot do.
This is how broken things
pile up inside of me and I keep walking,
calling out, "I love you. Come to me
because I cannot come to you."

Why the River is Always Laughing

The white spiders have fallen like blossoms;
or the other way around (equally true).
But whatever the pale travelers have been
they are melting like good days
into grasses where the green green turtle wakes
alone
in a certain season
and wonders where and what is this
whiteness drifting into shadow beneath him.
If I put my face down there among the blades
smelling of death and sun
and the sexual yearning that binds them,
the light creatures that have loved me
and are the only love I have given
fade from me also and descend
and become all there is to stand upon

or kiss. This is what the turtle finally sings about
and the beautiful spiders
and the grass changing to a spray of lamps
(and back) before you know.
This is the untranslatable obsidian book
that reads itself. And this is why
the river is always laughing, even when you drown,
even when you want, more than anything, to drown
and every river lets you live.

JON DAVIS

"Perfect Landscapes, Rich Branches of Blossom"

It is your world to make
and you choose to fill
rooms with necessary objects:
a Chinese vase, a painting of a woman
arranging flowers by moonlight,
a book of poetry by Basho.

A rose leans, revealing its moist stamen
within a halo of fragrance.
Why not a Spanish guitar
leaning in a sunny corner?
Why not music: Villa Lobos
or Rampal and his sentimental flute?

Your women are French, Oriental,
your men—artists, dancers, poets.
Don't you see? Even love
is a luxury. And now you have
cactus blooming in the sun room,
an oriole chirping from the flowering plum.

Someone is quoting Garcia Lorca.
A man wearing white silk,
a woman in a dress of pale cotton:
they sit at a wicker table,
in wicker chairs, looking away,
thinking in image, not word.

In this luxury of sun
they hold crystal goblets
filled with the glittering rosé
of thin blood. They kiss,
the nature of their desire revealed
by his restraint, her surrender.

Later, when they make love,
she recalls Nijinsky, turning,
his eyes, his shoulders, softening.
He thinks of Degas: his girlish ballerina
practicing: imagining each smooth stroke
along the flushed inner thigh.

White Body, Green Moss

I.

South of the river,
on the flood plain
I walk each evening,
cranes lope through saw-grass
and blunt-headed fish
rise in murky pools,
the late sun spreads
a thin film of light
across the calming waters
and olive trees gather
the thousand swallows
for the long flight.
There, beneath those trees,
the speaking began:
a voice without location

filled my bones,
yet seemed to rise
from the marrow.
It was a sound so deep
it set bushes ablaze;
mountains lifted and swirled
and faces loomed
until I knew that voice
was the voice of God.

II.

My son was sleeping, the rough white cloth
riddled with shadows as the sun struck
through our only window. I have only known
this impossible world—our burnished sun
rising from its lake of color, the thick wind
that blows all night, the howling wolves
and the deep pond of a woman's flesh.
He was sleeping; I woke him.
His long lashes fluttered like my hands
as I lifted him from the bed,
the bed of burning straw. I thought:
the beast inhabits my eyes, lurks
in the dark between words. And I lifted him,
just six years old, and held him
as he looked out from his dream.
I stood him on the floor; he looked at his feet.
I laced his sandals, and when he spoke
I knew the deed would be done.

III.

While vultures carved their spirals
into winds raised by the sun, its word for *heat*
rising visibly from the sand, we walked.
Near dusk, we reached the mountains
and he dropped onto the cool moss—*his white body
wrapped in white on the green moss.* I turned away,
prayed for strength, unwrapped the knife.
My son slept, his hand draped over his face,

87

his legs warm and twitching. A fly
hovered over his bare shoulder;
olive leaves shivered with wind, were still.
I raised the knife, and as I did, I looked up
and saw, flying over the single line of black mountains,
two figures, and I heard them call: two violent syllables.
They they were above us, the two of us—
father and son, and they called again, and again,
the notes I took for words.
                              Today,
walking south of the river, I remembered those figures—
wide, dusky wings flapping, necks of carved ivory—
and I knew that I had seen the birth of a new language,
new hope for this singular world, a new word for dust,
or sun, or the thick wind that rages all night.
                              I placed

the knife on the white cloth, wrapping it slowly.
I did not wake my son; I did not speak.
Now, I no longer hear voices.
I stand beneath the olive trees
and watch the sun plunge into the desert,
and I remember an affliction that seemed an ecstasy,
the knife in my hand uplifted, the white body,
green moss. Even the wind
stilled for my perfect witness.

PART TWO

Private History

"Growing up, father gave me a story about himself: in his heart of hearts he had always been a
writer"

James Hathaway

ALAN CHONG LAU

Origins

1

by the river
they built huts

faces caked with mud
walking on hands and knees

pictures drawn in the earth
with fingers and toes
and the words were never wrong

they would nod by fire
cracking branches like music
tunes the mountain sent them

faces
the eyes of wanderers
ears hung flappy
as fat mushrooms

lips uncomfortable
in just one place
would begin moving
seeds spread to wind

one morning nothing
only pieces of fingers lips
soft chunks of lobes
threads of hair in the water

huts
mere crumbs of ash
sprinkle the sand with birthmarks
snakes of smoke slither
thru tufts of grass

for the first time one looks at sky
expecting rain

2

the crows
return
dotting the shore
with slivers of noise

boys with slingshots
come down and kill
every single one

the water is bitter
clouds sour at the touch

barely scratching the mud
it runs in one thin trickle

the bodies of crows
mingle there
where it stops
making a pile of feathery flowers

A Chinese Landscape Painting in California—18?

for David Izu, painter

I see my family:
father washing bok choy in icy water
sits a straw hat on a rock

grandmother
a suspension of baskets defines the shoulders
red mud to reinforce a sluice

mother chasing down a chicken
wields an object resembling a cleaver
a lucky coin embedded at handle's end
catches a glint of sun

still asleep in long grass, a sister,
buds of flowers peek out of a tiny fist

overhead flocks of raucous birds
that don't speak our language
in fluent chinese i am yelling,
"papa, papa, what are those birds saying?"

not seen on the extreme right
a group of miners
coming to levy taxes on our life
whiskey on their breath
curls the clouds

there is no gold
in these surrounding hills
but how were we to know?

in a lower righthand corner
under dense foliage
the artist leaves his name
in branches of blood

i read the caption
in the catalogue
looking for some explanation
and find:

"by now
the sierra
has eroded this all
to dust riding wind"

LEO ROMERO

The Moon and Angels

I remember once as a child
traveling at night
and watching the moon

It is following me, I thought
It is my own guardian angel
like the one pictured
in the catechism books

All holy things glow
The stars, the sun
the moon and angels
Celso, I thought to myself
you are someone special
What have you done to make
the moon follow you like a dog

And I remember that
I had been to confession that day
and when I walked out of the church
the world was different
clearer, a little like heaven

When I had walked into the church
my heart had felt
like a dirty, ragged bag
filled with drowned kittens
But when I walked out the door
my heart was buoyant
afloat in the air
higher than any bird

That must be it, Celso
I thought
The moon is attracted
to the pure silver
of your heart
untarnished by sin

And I reasoned that the moon
was the halo of an angel
looking down from heaven
and thus could be seen
the top of his head

The Miracle

Celso had a vision
He saw the face of Jesus
on the wall of a small house
by the church in Agua Negra
He would pass by there each night
on his way home from the bar
usually so drunk on wine
that he would see two of everything
And in fact he saw two Jesuses
though he knew there was but one

By next day everyone had heard
of Celso's vision
That night there were hundreds of people
from the many mountain villages
gathered to see the miracle
Some say they saw the face of Jesus
others saw Satan, Mary, a Lamb
a Cross, and one little girl
even claimed to see the Last Supper
Those who saw nothing were quiet

Holy Water

For Easter, Celso put a sign
by the river reading
HOLY WATER—50 CENTS A BUCKET FULL
People were suspicious at first
How can you make such a claim
they would say
eyeing the river doubtfully

I had the priest bless the river
Celso would say
And now and forever
the flowing water of this river

95

will be holy water
but only between these two stakes
And Celso would point to two sticks
twenty yards apart

That is only as far
as the priest walked
before he fell into the river
and drowned thus becoming a saint
It is only while the water
is between these two stakes
that it is holy

BETH BENTLEY

Looking Back

I don't know what made me dream
you were a child again, except
finding that old photo in which
you're four years old and smiling,
eyes masked by the shadow
of your glasses, mysterious as a raccoon.

In my dream you're older
and the smile's become so knowing,
the folds of your mouth tuck it
primly in. Though I quailed and questioned,
you led me as if you were the parent
down an unlit hallway narrow as a foot-bridge
where I dared not look around
at cries and wrestlings, alarming
thuds from somewhere nearby.
Then, without warning, you were gone,
the way grown-ups suddenly leave
children they believe they have led

out of danger. And I woke up trembling,
the blind animal of my heart frantic.

Now you've sent me a poem from
my mother's house, about an old snapshot
taken when I was a child. You describe
my grandmother, mother, brothers
and me at a nameless lake.
You fit yourself into this cycle
of innocence and experience, trying
to interpret what the children's
veiled eyes conceal.

Sean, I would like to say
we're both safe onshore, beyond violence
or sorrow, that we protect each other
by the power of willing good—which is only
another way of naming love.
But I know better. The children's eyes
know better. They say the dark bridge
is always there; they say we must brave it,
child, mother, child; they say
looking back into each other's eyes
can steady us, the way
a paper boat is nudged and steadied
across a flood-creek-bed by someone
kneeling on the bank, holding a birch twig;
he leans out over the water, wand
tight in his hand, which does not waver;
the vessel tips and then is righted,
rallying in the swell and spin:
for a moment even the birds pay attention.

The Country Boy

In Memory of Theodore Roethke

Was it their voices
riding the family range

97

from baritone to soprano,
humming like bees,
that pulled you from room to room
hunting for treasure?

It seemed a safe, aimless sound,
hardly a tune,
and you either followed it
or it followed you on your rounds,
until you knew each other by heart.

The screen door orchestrated sooty overtures
to the fly on the grid,
a counterpoint in blue.
Or the rain talked to the windows
about something darker outside.

Later they found you stunned
before the impassive rectitude of winter,
knee-deep in stillness,
as if chained to the fence,
before you shook yourself and laughed
and, to everyone's relief,
made the snow sing the song you had made for it.

In spring the creek elucidated
what the faucets had merely implied.
You crawled closer on bruised knees.

Alone or not alone, there was nothing
to do but listen.
There were all those questions
only the grass could answer.

Though nothing was free;
you preferred your temperature
like a barefooted man hoping for shoes,
striking bargains.

They thought you might start a fire
in the dry fields, or break the stalks
on one of your headlong plunges.

The tinder under your coat
and the noise, that by now
none of them could avoid hearing,
made them uneasy.

Was the house glad when you left?
The attic, strewn with the bones
of nestlings and mice,
didn't believe in tears.
Downstairs the old one whispered,
"Wind's rising,"
They fastened the shutters.

WENDY BARKER

Black Sheep, Red Stars

He'd appear like a bird
that wanders into a place
on its way between two continents.
Surrounded by houses
that sopped up sparkle like sponges
he'd roll out of a '47 black Cadillac

and wave a bottle of rum
shimmering in the sun like amber.
"Pam, darling," he'd call to my mother,
his voice so raucous
Mrs. Simonitch next door
would move one slat of her Venetian blinds.

His toes pushed from limp *huaraches*
and he grinned as if he knew
just how much acid
the sight of him
shadow-bearded, yellow under the arms,
produced in my father's stomach.

99

When he talked
our windows grew arches, opened doors
onto courtyards, lemon trees, parrots,
we could hear the rustling of green feathers,
the chirrings and cawings of orange birds.
Small on the sofa I said

"Let me come live with you,"
something in my lungs knowing
that in a place named Jlayacapan
people might swallow drinks
the colors of bougainvillea
and move at night

to music that had never heard
of a metronome.
And when Uncle Dick and his friend Pedro
sat me between them
on the Cadillac's dusty front seat
to watch *High Society* at the Frontier Drive In,

I held myself taut and sweaty, dreaming stars
thicker than sugar on oatmeal,
stars farther than heaven,
stars and hibiscus and mangoes
that could cluster around a life
as long as a laugh.

The Navy Blue Chair

Wraps quiet in its smooth chintz,
silent as a rabbit,
as the black dazzle of midnight.

Outside the kitchen a Phoebe
sits on three eggs
as I rinse the omelet pan.

The chair's fabric
is slick as an egg, the chair
knows nothing of bloodshed.

Has no need for language.
Only—there is something
in the easy curve

of the firm high back
that might allow anything, anything
at all: hatching, feathering,

rising through dark air
with the lilt of a Mozart sonata,
the lift of a perfect souffle.

After the dishes are finished
I want to sit down. If I sit
long enough in the blue chair

I may know when the Phoebe's young
will crack through to the air,
when the summer storms will break—

when the clashing of flesh and beak,
the loud pounding of hard rain,
of hard flight,

will have to begin.

Teeth for Teeth

The leucojum, white bells with one green spot on the edge
    of each petal, bloom in the Berkeley hills from black clay
sponge-wet in the rain of gray January, February,
each flower the size of a tooth, white like teeth.

Like ghosts. We show our teeth. Camouflage
the red pulp of the tongue, red nerves in the eyes.

If we could drop one tooth every seven years like a seed,
drop that small whiteness into the soil
    so the moon could twist
its length into roots, white under dark, while above ground

101

the moon could be pulling and pulling at the single
seed,

pulling the tooth up to the night,
  winding black/green tendrils
around stars so that by sunrise you would know
where the ghosts of all old friends had gone,
  whirling in white
galaxies, waiting for the moment when teeth

bite blood, bite the dirt, anything but more whiteness,
anything to prove that all ghosts are alive.

TOM PARSON

Onion Soup

I wanted to start with the difficulty, solitude,
betrayal, isolation & name every
possible disagreement, what was said
that twisted my intention, & why . . .

start with a hot fire, with anger
I wanted to name ingredients, the recipe
the division of labor, the hunger, disunity
that I might turn in a moment to sudden advantage

I wanted to title the poem OPEN MARRIAGE:
footstep in the next room, stranger to me . . .
I wanted to write an inscription: sweet & sour

green pepper, pineapple, stir-fried . . .
I wanted to invite you both into the shower
but there are some things we just don't say to each other

Natural Birth

In a hurry to get into this world
on your first day you fly
from your mother by helicopter
from doctor to doctor
gulping pure oxygen.

I think how natural
even calamity is in this world:
I was born, I have been
told, foot first
though I can't remember
that first step.
It's a fact that some of us
don't use our heads.

There are many perhaps like myself
who have learned finally to say wait,
have patience, there is time enough
but already you know
you won't wait

already you know like no one else
the raw taste of air over Long Island Sound
& the urgent noise of people & machinery lifting your
four pound weight

a bottle with a plastic hose
bleeding sugar
into your arm

already you know the intricate connections
of this world:
to shake loose this poem for you
I imagine the natural wisdom that will show
on the edge of your first smile

DEL MARIE ROGERS

Family

"The words want to bring back more—" Charles Simic.

I want to bring back my grandfather, Richard Thomas,
tamping pipe tobacco with a big, worn thumb,
his battle-worn tomcat Pixie, nobody else's lap-cat,
dozing on his knees. Sun on the radio.
Or standing in the dim tool shed, under the apricot.
Getting up at five in the morning
to make smelly bait, to boil coffee.

I'm not thinking only of him.
I am thinking of myself,
I want the sun through branches heavy with apricots,
so slow there is no word for time.
Or the grape arbor whose intricate knots
wrapped the back screened porch.
I slept in a tangle of leaves.

Uncle Dick, they called him, in Chickasha, Oklahoma.
He was once mayor of a small town,
knew how it felt to lose everything—
property, money in the Great Depression.
His first wife, Pearl Grey, part Chickasaw,
left their baby, Toy, behind,
ran away to another life.

I'll search for words or my children won't know
he endured the worst of it,
stood quiet and steady.
They've never seen anything like that:
long winters of staying alive.
What will my children say about me?
I was the one who wrote this down.

He knew how to break new ground. Married
   my grandmother,

104

a frightened 19-year-old bride in a flowering hat,
fathered two more daughters, Opal,
   and my mother, Jewel.
In another photograph, his black eyes
pierce the walls around his life
as a gold miner in the Klondike
to ours, this room.

My sweet grandmother, Myrtle Roseberry, tight-lipped,
sewed by the window, thimble flashing,
put all her daughters through college.
She held on to all she loved
with stumps among the good, skillful fingers,
the missing ones lost in an accident with an axe
when she was a girl.

She braided her hair with those agile stumps,
weaving the triple stream of hair
like a girl's. Each day more white
crept into her iron-grey weaving,
the hair grown thinner.
She sewed by the window
until there was no more light.

Letter to My Mother

Birds, wind, grass. It's all I know.
It's enough. I've lost my old anger.
If I try to tell about the green
it's too much, each broad leaf
farther than my mind can reach,
a country of sun.
There's a danger I'm eccentric, strange—
I follow my life like a streak of luck.
I didn't know it would be so full
of surprises, turnings.
I am happy. I will live in a tree.
You won't understand, either, but maybe closer
than anyone else. A white egret stands

on a dead branch, in the marsh,
just about eye-level,
looks at me out of my strange past.

KATHLEEN CAIN

White Line

I think the day the radiator blew
in the middle of Kansas
is what started it. You were always willing
to go into the wilderness unprepared.
Something in you needed proving
that way, again and again. You should have
been John the Baptist, nothing but
honey and locusts all your days.
You'd have loved it,
and what a story to tell
once you got back home to me and the boy.
And that delicious young girl
who wanted to dance
with your head on a platter (you'd over-
heard her talking, that's when you planned
your escape, faithful and complete . . .).

It was that radiator.
I never trusted you after that.
Any man who'd cross Kansas
at the end of July
with a leaky radiator
just can't be trusted.
You knew it, too.
I watched your hand go from
tapping on the car door
in time to the wind

106

to that tight clutch of fingers,
uneven, slamming down
when the radiator, sucked dry
as a bone, pulled us down with it.
Nope. It was a small thing.
But I never trusted you after that.

The Lesson

for my great uncle John Crawford, still in exile from
Ballylanders, County Galway

Pride got passed at the breakfast table
along with the toast and the eggs.
It was served up cold.
It rolled in on high waves.
It got caught in the undertow of the brogue.

I thought we were in for an early story.
When I hammered at my hard-boiled egg
he said

> that's good, that's good—
> eat it all, eat it all

1916.   Something called *The Rising*.
The egg slid out of its shell.
I held the toast suspended.
Only eleven, I was just getting breasts.
I couldn't, even with my eyes closed,
imagine 1916. By the time I opened
them, I knew he was talking about war.
All the men in our family
have been at war sometime or another.
Now it was exile. No going back.

> exile is just too much talk that raises visions
> anyway

he said

I can remember my mother
and the yellow corn meal
that came to Ireland
all the way from Minnesota . . .

I finished the toast
while he talked about the Black and Tans
in a too calm voice. They sounded like
the Germans to me.

No. Worse, he said.
Worse.

I could hear his steps then
clattering on a stone street.
His breathing heavy and hurting.
Other steps. Clattering too.
All a scratching scraping surface.
The cell in a jail I'd know
if I could just remember the name.
Not Long Kesh. Maybe Kilmainham.
Eleven years.
He counted every bar and stone
that lined the floor and walls.
He knew daylight by its single thread
on the floor, envied spiders
that crawled out between the spaces.
When crumbs were thrown he wet the tip
of his finger and pressed it to cover,
like he did now his plate,
the inches of stone for fragments of bread.

JAMES HATHAWAY

Private History

Growing up, father gave me a story
about himself: in his heart of hearts

he had always been a writer,
but he had lost his best work somehow—
left it on a table at the student union,
forgetting everything in the heat of some
minor argument, or given it to a careless
student, who had gone on unconsciously
to law school and was never heard from
again. Or perhaps the kindly janitor, trying
to neaten up father's chaos of old coffee
and small press trash, had thrown it out,
mistaking it for all that unwanted paper.
He wasn't sure, but such things naturally
happen. They might not have made him famous,
who knows, still they were his favorite
poems. I naturally never believed
such stories: in my heart of hearts
I knew this kind of thing was always
imaginary. I was cruel: it was expected.
As a child, I knew I was strange, "unnatural"
as father's friends would say, more interested
in bugs and rocks than people. I remember
a mossy creek I loved to play in, rooting
for salamanders and crayfish under the slimy
rocks, at peace with myself amid the trickle
of water and the green shade. I thought
the deep gorge and the big trees seemed ancient
and holy and not until college did I learn
where this comes from. I remember later
how I went back to this place to find the special
cliffs, the still pools, but all was changed
and shrunk and overgrown. It was wet and smelled,
but not as I remembered. Once, when I was
in graduate school, I told this story in a bar,
to a bunch of weasel-faced friends,
and they laughed, and I drunkenly admitted
that sometimes I thought I had inherited
Wordsworth's soul—a big mistake. I remember
father too, one evening, having drunk too much,
complaining about the lost work, how it would
never ever come again, knowing that he was
saying too much, but wishing that he could

say more, do more, make us see and believe.
He was inconsolable.

Perfume

It comes back to me, walking today
among the late season bushes,
almost beyond blooming, this strong perfume
she used to use. I liked it a lot
and used to spend even necessary
food money to buy her more, to keep
the illusion going, because it was rich
with complex dying, like old gardenias,
like the last supernatural season
in the fatally blighted garden where
black mold grew on roses sticky sweet
with aphids and because the honor of
sharing such an ineffable beauty
was a real thing to me then.
It's occurred to me more than once since
that I am prone to this, like cancer
or heart disease, an excess of sentiment
or a chemical imbalance, if you prefer,
that comes on suddenly—
say, seeing three vague birds
move across the suburban sky, cutting
from dark into light, or watching
an injured ball player sob on the tv,
while I eat dinner with the evening news.
These days, I need an inner doctor to tell me
to refrain from such heady odors,
and then keep to a simple, honest diet:
the rank healthy smell
an old pot roast makes reheating,
the sharp tinge of pesticide the garden
needs for treatment, to keep living.

110

ROSEMARY CATACALOS

Tongue-Tied

I am drunk and alone again
in your house,
this place with so many mirrors.
You have gone for food,
leaving me helpless against
these reflections on all sides.
Everywhere the air
is covered with our imprint,
with what is forbidden
and also what is not forbidden.
I can only give in
and try to write this.
A stranger arrives
and sits in the next room
wondering why I won't speak.

All I have ever
been trying to do is speak.
It's just that sometimes
I'm an angel
with far too many names.
They clog my lungs and tongue
with their possibilities.
They keep me in a room apart.
They set me spinning into mirrors.
The names you call me by.
Sister. Lover. Teacher.
The names the others
have given me.
Our Lady of the Miraculous Hands.
Our Lady of the Tainted Corners of Time.
Our Lady of the One Word
    We all Know But Cannot Say.
Mother of the Ferocious Teeth.

Mother of the Six Seeds of Spring.
Mother of Hearts Waiting
   By the Sides of All Roads.
Ariadne of the Treacherous Thread.
Ophelia Who Died for Our Sins.
Phoenix. Venus.
Even just plain Demetres' daughter.
I have answered
to all these names and more.
And there are others still to come.

I suppose there is no reason
to say these things.
Except this house
is so full of mirrors.
And a stranger has arrived
and sits in the next room
wondering why I won't speak.

Ariadne To Dionysios

We have hiked hours to get to this place. Around
seven coves, over stones, past the blue and orange
boats, the thick smoke of the fishermen's fires.
Nothing stands between us now. Now we know
what it is to be on an island. Nothing stands
between us and the *sea*, Dionysios.

Earlier, when you sat hunched in the cafe over
syrupy black coffee in a tiny cup, did you think
then of pressing your lips to my throat? When you
stood at the window at night plucking the lyre.
Was I there as the curtains blew in
from the sea? There in the familiar rubbing of
the grandmothers' homespun on your hard forearms?
Even before, when you lay in all the red and purple
beds of Asia, did you think about my breasts?
That they are the fruit of the sacred vine?
The way I would delight again in twining

around your famous staff if you could only
get me into the sun long enough?

Oh, Nyounios, I've come back to you at last. Here
where the rough shore is the simple bedclothing
of the sea. Here, where in the forgiving eye of the fire
that begot you, you tenderly unwind the final thin cloth
of my tunic. Here where you ride me like a dolphin, half
in, half out of the water. Your teeth, ancient shells,
imprinting my skin. Here where you drink so deep from
the wild cup of my wine. Your eyes so much like my eyes.

Sometimes I'm still afraid. You know that.
I am, even if a princess, a simple weaver
of spells. Sometimes of faith that
there will be no more mazes, no more beasts.
But hold me, Nyounios. We are marking time
with our bodies, our old ties, Here there will be
no abandonment except to the pleasure of one
another. We have crowned ourselves and are moving
three times around the stone altar that is this
island, this first and only island.

Poison In The Eye Of The Beholder

1

For some time now the hot brown city
has been impotent to touch me
except to call up disgust.
I am impatient with stooped old men
who take too long crossing streets.
I am unable to transform them.
They are embarrassing, graceless.
They are doing nothing but dying.
I grit my teeth at the regularity,
the sameness with which they
shuffle haltingly away to
pathetic rooms of faded gray

boards that lean and rot as they do.
They arrive to emptiness or perhaps
there are children and grandchildren
who shove them into corners.
Many must go home to wives whose
lips move incessantly, noiselessly;
whose eyes even in sleep are
rolling toward the grave,
whose knees bleed crosses on the floors,
who don't bother with shoes anymore because
they will never again leave their houses
or their constant prayers for death.
They send the old men out
to the corner stores for whatever
is needed to barely get by.
They send the old men out to drink
and act as scouts, as divining rods,
to attract the ghosts of dead mothers
and brothers and sisters.
The old men with their lives
coming loose from their bones.
The old men who don't remember,
whose days have matted together
like their dirty yellowed hair.
The old men always spitting
their untold stories into the dust.
The old, men and women, who are all the time
shuffling and praying and dying,
sores on the filthy skin of the world.

2

Ancianos, forgive me.
All my life you have given me
songs and lessons and hope.
And now because I let myself turn
ugly, I fix you with a dead stare.
The love has gone out of my seeing.
Now because I have lost my way,
lost what you taught me to celebrate,
I betray you.

114

Ancianos, forgive me this failure.
You are innocent of it.
I do not deserve you.
It is I who have died badly.
I am the carcass,
the empty shell whose eyes and wings
and heart have been eaten away by ants.
Ancianos, if you will have me
I will follow the light in your faces
back to life,
and in time I might be worthy
of a death as proud
as the one you move toward
leaning on your sticks of courage,
singing into what is at the
other side of the morning.

LEROY QUINTANA

Cross a River

Cross a river it was leeches
Hear a company of NVA's crashing towards you
    would be a troupe of baboons
A green snake named Mr. Two Step
    for the number you'd take after bitten
Was said the NVA's carried flashlights
    One night frightening scores of them
    turned out to be a swarm of fireflies
The whirr of birds' wings
    was artillery rounds
Threw stones at a poised cobra once
    as the sun going down. Fire it up
    and the VC would know our position
A VC moving slowly in the elephant grass

115

happened to be a water buffalo
One night they overran the compound. Loaded down
   with grenades, AK 47's. From North Vietnam.
   Mines strapped to their chests.
   These only the mosquitoes
Called in the new Cobras
   The VC only a whisper away
   Came in striking twice the death
   as the old gunships
Was also said the VC kept chickens leashed to strings
   So easily frightened they were perfect warning
   One night, shivering uncontrollably with fear
   knowing I would have to kill whatever was out there,
   walking slowly, scratching

There Was Always A Sadness

There was always a sadness in the joy
of Doña Marina's visit. She was grandma's friend,
the vecina from across the street
Over coffee they would mention the weather,
a death on our side of town
but always the talk turned to their sons
A picture of grandma's son on the wall behind her
the Stars and Stripes waving proudly in the background
her eyes moist as she mocked MacArthur in Spanish
It was easy for him to say he would return
He was a general and never suffered
They'd sit for a while in silence, console one another
The mothers Pedro Infante sang about in that sad song
about a young man, sad that he must leave his mother
entrusting her to la Virgen de Guadalupe
as he goes off to prove he too can die for his country
Doña Marina's son never knew combat
Came home one summer on leave from Basic Training
impressed us doing chinups on his front porch
and just as quickly gone and Doña Marina always

116

after that telling grandma about the sparrows playing
on the ledge of the hospital window the day he died

vecina—neighbor

DON ERON

Acorns

Acorns falling to the street all night
kept me awake. My father sat by my bed
until I slept. These acorns keeping everyone
awake, he'd shake his head, including neighbors
with oak trees hanging over their driveways
(I liked to throw at them in the day)

and children old enough to read newspapers.
I read the newspaper. There was the man
gunned down by burglars on the steps
of the Hamburger Palace at 4 in the morning.
You didn't have to be a child to know
next they were coming for us. I could hear

their footsteps on the stair. *Acorns,* said my father.
But he couldn't *swear* they wouldn't. He sat
by my bed until I slept. It wasn't until years later
that I saw 4 in the morning. When I did,
it was with vengeance. If somebody
wanted to gun me down, they were welcome.

This was about a woman. This woman
resisted my attentions, I was sorry, the usual story. . . .
It can all be put simply. Something to lose sleep over,
that cuts deeply, that soon would send me
walking the streets at 4 in the morning.
It was better to take it moving

117

than the twist and turn routine.
   People who saw me coming
would cut across the street. An entire year spent
in a Hopper painting, I had nothing
to show for it. And I thought I should. That I could sleep
again was hardly enough. The woman
   still would have nothing
to do with me. It's easy

to be cavalier about such suffering—to even
   call it *suffering*
affronts language, Mandelstam
whispering last poems near Vladivostok, Miklos Radnoti,
Paul Celan. The list in this century alone lingers
long as the century. What can you do with it? You don't
have to be up at 4am to walk outside

and see the wheelchairs. Or read the newspaper once. If
it was easy to be cavalier about myself, that in two years
when somebody asked me her name, I came up blank
still doesn't mean it wasn't real enough. I don't know
   how my father
got through those next days, he must have been so tired.
I remember his name was Kavanaugh. In 1962

Kavanaugh was gunned down
on the steps of a Hamburger Palace. He was 27.
Just off the night shift. But even if
they'd found his killers
the story wouldn't change for a boy of 9.
He'd hear killers on the stair, and then he'd sleep.

Italy

He stood in Ravello watching the sea.
Women, work, family—
none of it connected with something
he'd seen, not tangibly, off Capri
yesterday. As if his soul held a thing

118

he didn't want or need, something fleet
that sliced his heart. It was hard to be-
have with it, is all he thought. But to see
within him now, watching the sea in Italy,
then to go home tomorrow as if he
was what he'd been still, always, though something
was slicing his heart so he couldn't breathe.
It was more than he wanted to believe.
He'd changed, not tangibly, he'd
had to be without—meeting
what he'd been without decorum, then yesterday leaving
Capri before he'd known the sea
within his longing. In Italy
he leaned to the wall of the sea.
What did it mean? He'd had epiphanies
before everywhere, and would sometimes believe
all would be different—though he
didn't need to be so different, was happy
enough, often, as he was. And now he'd
stood by a wall in Italy
watching the sea. Something fleet
sliced his heart. He'd be what he'd be,
given, Ravello, anywhere, yet he'd
live with this fleet thing, he'd
bring what he could to these things
he loved. But would they be easy,
too, like watching the sea
or meeting, yesterday, what he'd been—take this sea
within his longing, changed as he,
already, for these things
he loved—would they too be this easy
as in nothing he'd given had ever been?

PHIL WOODS

The Little Tramp Goes to Spain

The two car rag-tag, rattle-tattle,
derail at any time, stop at every
one house town (car's seats all taken up
by draftee mountaineer
soldiers)
      snaked along & I thought I'd
have to toss my cookies. If it weren't
for the Goya beauty singing
"Norwegian Wood" in Spanish to her
crippled boyfriend, time would have stood still
& I'd still be on that train—A life sentence.

Canfranc/ End of Line. Pine silhouetted
valley. Victorian era station instantly
deserted upon arrival. Nary a
toilet to be found.
Crossed bridge to
go to village. I became
Charlie Chaplin—a conspicuous
toilet roll in hand. Two guardia
civil. Black Mickey Mouse Hats. Machine
Pistols. Tough Talk. Passports Pronto!
I fumbled. Confused. Almost asking
Mr. Cop to hold my roll while I dug
out Papers. *Heat* loosened up. Even
they saw how ludicrous it was & besides
we were Americans: you know, Bases, financing,
joint maneuvers.

Between touristy alpine buildings we
threw down our bags among the pines.
All night the dream / rifle
butts & barrels / awakening
to black jack boots / The legacy

part comic opera. Franco's face
still on the money. I had
to get out of there.

Fathers And Sons

In a dream my mother and
I are consoling each other
in an alternative version
of my father's funeral.

In the dream world
these events have their own life,
their own pattern of grief.

One awakens disturbed,
experiencing it all, again.
I can picture it still:
Three o'clock in the morning,
Dumas, Texas.
We are unable to sleep
in the shabby motel
hearing every semi-truck
shift gears & roar off.

So Dad & I get up,
go off to an old diner,
order a greasy breakfast
& talk.

I can see his face, now,
staring at me,
full of inquisitiveness,
trying so hard to connect.

I couldn't let him in.
I'd just cracked up
and was hanging on
by a thin thread.

Two American men,
father and son,
both wiped out
by the American scene.

So, he starts telling me
old Air Corps stories
from his young manhood
in the Big War,

a couple of new ones that
I was too tired to remember.
He apologizes for telling them
and calls himself dumb.

I say, "No, don't do that.
You don't have to apologize.
I've always liked hearing
your stories."

We both grow quiet.
It is a moment I'd
like to have back.
I'd hug him and

tell him the truth.
Maybe not. That's the way
it is with fathers & sons.
They can't ever get down to it.

There he was,
adrift in memory,
hungry for love & for
some way to make sense of it.

I see, now, his story
and its ending
he saw coming
even then.

And, there I was—
his rebel son
clenching my teeth
to choke down

122

the madness
that engulfed me
when I came back
from Europe

and couldn't adjust
to being back
and to seeing so clearly
the dark collective

insanity behind
the smiling face
of the American Dream—
Barbara Walters interviewing
cancer ridden John Wayne as
the Shah fell in Tehran,

the same demonic
forces that exterminated
Indians & rationalized
slave ships gathering
feverishly, again,
in the American psyche.

So, quite often I sit
in a red vinyl booth
in Dumas, Texas,
with my father

trying to imagine
how that last conversation
could have gone differently.

JUDITH SORNBERGER

My Father Sells the Homeplace in the Sandhills

My grandmother calls crying and he's gruff.
She has no right to make him feel
so bad. He tells me she's been bad
each time she's called. Bad,
the way she was when Grand-dad died
and she wouldn't be consoled for anything.

An old house is an old house after all.
His past belongs to him now,
not to her or to that house.
It's likely any day now to fall down.
Why is she behaving like a child?

He thinks if he does not tell it
I will forget his story:
how each day in summer, hearing
the train whistle, he jumped
into the saddle duded up,
climbed the hill across the track
to wave passengers west by cowboy hat.

Having offered himself as symbol
standing on that hill, he thinks
now he can just take himself back,
dissolve his image in the eyes
of children who tugged at mother's sleeves:
Look, a real cowboy. He waved at me.

Suppose that cowboy is the only thing
to stand up to the hills and plains
along a flat day's ride through memory.
And suppose it is the only way I have
of seeing him besides suited and tied,
driving away each day of my childhood.

Returned from the last visit,
the closing on the house,
he waves away my mentioning it.
His hand like the hand of the boy
leaving the saddle horn
to brush away a fly buzzing his face,
while the other holds so lightly to the reins,
it forgets that it is holding anything.

Visit

Now is the time for coyotes
to stop crying in our ears;
to sell the Sandhills home
and lose the town: its cattle
history, the hills, the hills.

Grandmother leads me to the quilts
folded on her mother's bed.
One for each grandchild, our births
predicted in the heavy winters
of her mother's labor. Choose,
she says, and there are no surprises,
no new patterns: stars,
the wedding ring, log cabin.

Sure, you remember Great-grandmother,
my mother insists. I don't, and try
reading her face in the yellowed newspaper.
Obituary calls her face a china doll's.
Mom says no, she was tough.
Killed a rattlesnake trespassing
in her garden with the cane
they all believed she leaned on.

Just as they supposed her husband her support
before his cutthroat suicide in their front yard.
And she had gone on folding down the quilt
from her small body each day before dawn.

Gone on feeding children
and chickens given children's names,
gathering eggs.

I try tracing the hand that struck the snake,
its knuckles coarsened against wind and burrs,
the grit under the nails from garden work,
in the only map I have of her,
the quilt I choose: star pattern.
Here to trace her veins in tiny stitches,
here to find her hands in five-point stars.

My last night in the Sandhills
the stars come out in patterns I look for
standing knee-deep in wet pasture.
Star chart against the sky, I turn
until I'm sure north points to north,
try piecing stars into stories I hold.
But it won't work. Stars out here
are close together as quilt stitches,
close in their vast distances as relatives.
The patterns I brought with me do not fit.

Perhaps she knew those myths,
their foreign names, but chose
to give the stars an order
she inherited from women's hands,
one closer to home. Now I squint
to see them through her needle's eye,
and looking must be sharper,
less detached. It is chilly here
at night even in summer, and I fold
around myself what she has left,
knowing its warmth was not meant for me.
But in the code of stitches
my fingers read her will
to cover all she loved, and I am covered.

BILL TREMBLAY

Rock From The Foothills

In my hands, the rock weighs
many generations, each grain a silicon person.
Inside its crack are the rooms
where we sweated orange from dye-vats,
hoisting huge rolls of parachute nylon.
Bright cones sway down sand-colored skies
to my aunt, viewing my mother's body in the coffin.
"She still looks like a spoiled brat," she says.

My grandfather, dead at 33,
from no child labor laws & tuberculosis & booze
trying to save his imagination singing vaudeville
made my mother his little queen, Irene,
& my Iroquois great-grandmother, "Le Sauvage,"
watched him cough his life out
& smoked her corncob & gave the evil eye
to the french-canadian idea that safe is good.

This rock sounds different
when hit by different memories.
My uncle's small fist makes a cancer sound;
a factory-whistle saying there's no other life
but in the mills
makes the sound of my aunt's children,
stillborn, knocking to get out.

The Hallucination War

In the small cove at San Pedro
coalseams fork like black silver shrouds
through rock. I trace orders of antediluvian fern
& the sound of the waves revives the old thirst
for a whiskey.

127

Down the strand, a stone column
breaks from the headland to stand alone
like an Easter Island face, staring forever skyward.
The cliff walls glint with bits of glass inset
in cement—seahorse, scallop, sailboat.

American music from the cafe
brings me up the steps. A line of warships
cruises out of Lisbon harbor. The radio says China,
invasion. Perhaps the final war
my sons are certain of has come & the earth
is going deliriously inside itself like a gypsy
seized with glossolalia.

In the wall, a little shrine
untenanted by any saint is hollowed out
with words inlaid of stone:
      ao deus desconbecido, it says,
        to the god unknown . . .
The sky is brittle like the inside of a kiln
lined with blue tile.

Creation

In school the nuns taught God
made the heavens and earth in six
days. Duhamel never believed it.
He saw his mother and father make it
in one day.
           At first it *was* dark.
His mother lifted the curtain and made
light shine through the glass windows
and the wooden crossbars, making their
children, the shadows.
              His mother
carried him and created the kitchen,
the bathroom, talcum, pleasure. She
made the air, the smell of hot toast.
His father walked him with both hands

128

and created doors, the world outside,
angel clouds, and telephone wires strung
above streets were how things're connected.
He created motion in a maroon Packard,
and colors for go, stop, and maybe.

They created smokestacks, steeples, and silos
to mark the different kinds of work.
They created Revere Beach and, for
everything without end, the Atlantic,
with waves rushing toward him saying,
"Reverse. Everything in reverse."

Darkness came: light in reverse.
Shouting came: laughter in reverse.
Duhamel invented more uses for darkness,
the pleasures of making the world over.
Bathrobe sky. Melted tar night. Packard wind.
He hummed as his eyes opened in reverse.

SANDRA CISNEROS

No Mercy

Your wives left
without a trace
both of them

they plucked
their long hair
from the kitchen sink
did not forget the ring
nor the domestic combs
not one stray stocking
did they leave

not a fingerprint

nor a subscription
to a favorite magazine

they fled

gathered their feathers
and bobby pins and string
left nothing

took their towels
and their initials
one child
expensive shoes

and vamoosed

without a clue

you must've said
something cruel
you must've done
something mean
for women to gather

all of their things

In a Red-Neck Bar Down the Street

my crazy
friend Pat
boast she can chug
one bottle of Pabst
down one swig
without even touching
teeth grip
swing and it's up in
she glugging like a watercooler
everyone watching
boy that crazy
act every time gets them
bartender runs over

says lady don't
do that again

MICHAEL HOGAN

Ernest Hemingway—1961

When the sun comes early
through eastern windows
and a single horsefly buzzsaws the air
it is then I rise from bed
my dreams of amputation, of teeth lost,
cloaked in the amnesia of another day
overwhelmed with trivia.

We make our own rules and lose by them.
This morning after a breakfast of coffee
and ice water I walk to the corner
feeling my liver dissolve in a
cacophony of stale beer and bad whiskey.
June drips a melody sweet as rose water
and the town wakes slowly.

These things are substance, Mary, not prelude.
Only what moves us has meaning.
The rest is lost in a weed-choked yard
or the gutter with brown cigarette butts,
orange peels, used condoms.
When words fail, the hammer drops.
Living can never be its own excuse.

I have carried this gun in dreams:
quiet ones in which a wounded animal
is given peace by the hunter's grace.
Now hunter and animal, I find myself
precipitating an act gentle as June rain.

And in this dazzling pellet-rain
I'll sing the best of all men's songs.

Take care, Mary, of the cats. Smile
at those who call me coward.
These last weeks so free of conflict
are quit also of energy and force.
I am become arbitrary as a moveable feast,
my life arbitrary, capricious as a poem of Pound's.
Only the gun gives me substance
this trigger my clearest, most careful line.

From a Hospital Window

So here I am in another place
no further in this movement
than a lifeboat taken out by the tide
passengers safe or not
to float for use, for salvage, or lost
in the turgid flow.
No accident either unless the double helix is
with its blind poet and deaf pianist.
Or always accidental
mistakes greening the earth like toads' eyes.

It is noon. One hundred and ten degrees.
In the fields across from my hospital window
workers take their lunch in the narrow shade of pickups.

They eat slowly, without speaking,
their brown backs and dusted pants
almost connected to the earth. I speak to them.
One has delicate hands, when younger
he dreamed of being an artist.
Another with the surly look of one who beats his wife,
complains of bad digestion.
One, it is apparent, drinks too much
from an old sorrow which carves
its tracery across his sunburned face.
Another speaks of the land as a woman.

132

It can be seen he is one with his work,
has never been ambitious for any other.

But, in fact, all of this is a lie.
I do not talk to them at all.
How could I? They out in the fields,
me behind a hospital window?
The field across the road
has been empty since dawn, thirsting for rain.
There is no life there to speak of.
Never is when you need it
to make the living easier.

Sand

—for Richard Shelton

Living is a temporary affair
a squatter's shack in Sabino Canyon,
bare ribs bleached like a paddle wheeler
lost on a sandbar.
Sometimes we act like it's forever:
burn brothers and bridal bouquets
in one great fire.
We chant *life life* circling the flames.
But flowers are dying all around us,
trees are burning.
In the crackling underbrush
even the rocks have melted.
Yet we go right on chanting,
circling the fire like moths.

One among us goes into the desert.
He finds the exact words,
knows whoever follows will understand.
Each letter formed perfectly as silicon.
But in August the rains come,
then dust devils and wind storms.
Those who follow find only these fragments:

. . . I go to sleep
but . . . never believe it.

They think they know precisely what this means.
They build great houses,
make plans to live forever.

CHARLES BEHLEN

Dogs

There was a small one
that coughed froth,
two big ones
(a brother and sister),
their piss-yellow hair
matted by days of
sleepy indigence.
They lived that way,
napping under my
grandmother's house,
panhandling for scraps,
milling the porch.

When he came to kill them
my uncle laid the 12 gauge
across his wide lap
and finished a beer.

My grandmother sat
under the wall phone.
Fingers in ears,
eyes shut tight,
she shouted SIT DOWN
AND BE QUIET
as I jumped from

window to window
and the soft pops
jostled the china.

A big yellow
lay on the road.
Its tail still wagged,
thrashed the gravel.
The others soaked
two gunney-sacks in the
back of the pickup.

While my grandmother
patted sweat from the
last of the six-pack
my uncle let me
shovel sand on the
moons of blood.

There was a buckshot wound
in the side of the wellhouse.
I fingered it, dreamed
of earning my keep.

On the Plains, in West Texas

the deer hung from the wellhouse rafter
where it twisted, frozen and alone
through the long push of wind,
the prairie winter.

When the white geese threaded out of the south;
when the chain on the flagless school house pole
broke free, whipped the cool air warmer; when
the ragged windbreaks of ugly elms rashed mint-green
and the March gusts burned the dust to the air,

I was given this:

to pry the wellhouse open with a hoe.
If the carcass was cold there was meat for three weeks;

if the neck-stump dripped maggots on the floor
I cut the deer loose, dragged it to the field
  and doused it with gas.

While the body burned open
I stood among the broken-necked stalks,
felt the sky change course, as the
geese trawled softly for a darker home.

RAY GONZALEZ

Desert or Dream

1

I don't know how many new galaxies
are created each night, but they allow
the family tree to stay embedded
in the adobe wall.
In one corner, we are angels.
In one kiva, we are gods.
I stand behind that explosion
to learn each thing from this Mexicano,
this brown body of the Indio hiking
across the desert that has spread over
his life for too long.

The weather gets hotter by degree,
but I can't grasp it among the sweat,
the salt in the eyes that reminds me
this is where my grandfather,
Bonifacio Canales, crossed the river
to cut throats for la revolucion Mexicana,
the spot where I can't find the right dust storm,
the hottest sand that hurts my feet,
a reminder to keep going and ask my grandmother

how much older do we have to grow
before knowing we have chanted
too many rosaries, answered too many prayers
by placing bare feet on the steaming sand.

2

This is how we tell each other tales
that have already happened,
conduct ceremonies that must be believed.
In the cottonwoods, old fires still command.
In the Rio Grande, los Mexicanos still drown,
but still come across.
In the adobe ruins, the oath is still carved
in blood on the walls.
On the cactus, the hand still suffers
the thorn at any cost.
In the canyons, the wisdom of rock is foremost.
In this desert that cannot be cast off,
the rocks, the sand, the rattlesnake,
and the scorpion still appear
like a wish always granted,
bite like greed always gained,
rule the path like the scorching sun
on brown skin, peeling it open like
the conquistador that tortures you.

3

My yearning in the desert is
tinged by a bloody history,
a chemical of smoke and sand mixed with
the ancient blood of those that were massacred
defending this hot, persistent land.
I keep coming back to the ruins because
my recurring dream leads me here,
to the battle and vision of how my tribe and pueblo
were defeated because I failed to sound the call
from the lookout cliff, failed to warn the family
and the fire has burned for centuries.
That dream leaves me inside the ruins that

refuse to disintegrate into the earth,
this black desert charred in a primitive time when
each of us could trace one path for the tribe,
for the dwelling, for the group thrown off
the bloody cliffs to haunt this desert until
the terror, somehow, is laid to rest.

4

Here is the way out of the vision
with its restless calling, so unashamed.
How do we find the final direction without
ancient hands to hold us, or lovers to arrest us?
How do we inhabit the pueblo with family that
will love, forever, and survive the intense heat
that hunts for the weakness of love?

Take the offering to mark the day.
Take the cathedral to the eye that worships
the vision, a pueblo of feasting with painful existence.
When the prayers are answered, new houses are inhabited.
Take the time it takes to give birth.
When the child is born, forget that fire.

Step between the two filaments in the heart.
Heat and dust, sun as giant god rewriting
the carvings on the walls, cracked by dust clouds,
filaments of worn stone,
the skin as a map lost in the canyons,
found burning where the heat took over.
New pillars of rock are left behind
as signposts to travelers:
this is where the pueblo burns in history,
this is where the heat and dust find and
feed the new savage,
this is where I turn back,
this is where the chanting begins.

I must go home, the heat persists.
I must go home, dirt roads are paved.
I must go home, rattlesnakes come out from the rocks.
I must go home, the cactus cuts the skin,

then blossoms with vengeance.
I must go home, more Mexicanos cross the border.
I must go home, canyons fill with rocks.
I must go home, it is still not the right dust storm.
I must go home, the family prays at the altar.
I must go home.

GREG GLAZNER

October Homecoming

—Midland, Texas

Fanfares and concession at the ballfield
as two grown boys come witnessing,
clean-palmed and shiney in their rings.
The tall one pities me with his eyes,
his rigid hands working at the dark,
the other turns up his face to feel more force
actual as bone, as pads crack, headgear,
and fists behind us rise by thousands.

The sense, in the sudden roar, disintegrates,
in the brass band's blunt pummelling,
in the fallout drifting white as hatred
from the stadium lights, into the open mouths.
I taste it turning from them hot along the sidestreets,
down the gravel roads, old rage,
an acid failure touched off far
into the imaginary desert night. Starfall,
the city a small, lighted sore, and in all directions
oil rigs lighted up like missiles. Snakefields,
black grass where local boys come wading.
Somewhere, slung with rifles, they hesitate,
bearing my hatred of them in their spotlight,

jackrabbits bounding endlessly out of range,
bits of glass needling the self-righteous, prodigal eye,
now a cottontail in that beam, white-blinded,
now twitching with a slug lodged in its brain.

Walking Two Landscapes

for Ann

1

I step out into the cold air
and watch chunks of snow
glint and drip from the pines.
I pick up a last birch leaf—
it's ice-crusted,
red-ribbed;
everywhere woodsmoke dissolving in clear light,
and knock two more sticks of wood together,
ice shattering in the sharp air.

The dry weeds, sunbleached, stiff,
resonate over an inch of snow.
Magpies settle
onto the fencerow, and call out,
and I know nothing to answer them.
They pace the rails, cackling,
glancing sidelong at me, and fly.
Flashes of my face
scatter in their black eyes.

2

Sweltering one summer in the Texas heat,
I gnashed my Baptist faith
until it snapped like a tether;
and walked the flat streets emptied.
Pecan trees waved the leaves
they might hold five more months,

and the thick skin of paint
cracked and scaled from the houses.
Wysteria blooms draped in clusters
from the fences, like blue
grapes I wanted to consume.
Know only the blooming when they fall,
I thought, smooth-faced and nineteen,
the wind already rushing past me
carrying all the years I'd live.

3

Under small, sharp-edged bits of light
which might have gone out centuries ago,
or which already have exploded
into novas our children
will live too soon to see,
we walk our frozen path to the mountain,
certain, for this night,
of the gentleness of stars,
as their gauzed light
drifts onto us, and rises again,
ghostly, in snowlight.

And under rough maples full of stars,
through crusted layers
where everything we love scars
its names across us
the way I cut mine in live oak,
for always, with my first lover's,
afraid, even then, of the day I'd be a liar—
we cut the old words a new way,
and sheets of thin light press into us,
and even the chill voice rattling the weeds,
rising, as if hearing our words,
to tell us *These you will
abandon, or die from,*
pushes us closer.

A horse loose from the stall
climbs ahead of us, head down,

black coat shined silver,
and trots into the clearing,
the night flowing perfectly
into the tatters of his mane.
He stands and looks
without desire,
without knowing what he sees,

and disappears into the trees again.
We glimpse the white ankles,
a piece of his back, and once,
his whole broad head. For minutes
the low branches rustle and break.

4

When it is silent
and the tall grass has given up
each sliver of warmth,
we stop, our breath lighting up,
the smell of pine sap
cutting the cold air,
and watch a few clouds drift over.

They ooze from their linked shapes,
slow, thick, as if they too had flowed
from a split in the crusted wood,
shadowing us as they pass
under the new moon,
now white-edged, blooming out of themselves,
now lungshaped and warm.

RAYMOND CARVER

The Cranes

Cranes lifting up out of the marshland . . .
My brother brings his fingers to his temples
and then drops his hands.

Like that, he was dead.
The satin lining of autumn.
O my brother! I miss you now, and I'd like to have you back.

     Hug you like a grown man
who knows the worth of things.
The mist of events drifts away.

Not in this life, I told you once.
I was given a different set of marching orders.
I planned to go mule-backing across the Isthmus.

Begone, though, if this is your idea of things!
But I'll think of you out there
when I look at those stars we saw as children.

The cranes wallop their wings.
In a moment, they'll find true north.
Then turn in the opposite direction.

Movement

Driving lickety-split to make the ferry!
Snow Creek and then Dog Creek
fly by in the headlights.
But the hour's all wrong—no time to think
about the sea-run trout there.
In the lee of the mountains
something on the radio about an old woman

who travels around inside a kettle.
Indigence is at the root of our lives, yes,
but this is not right.
Cut that old woman some slack,
for God's sake.
She's somebody's mother.
You there! It's late. Imagine yourself
with the lid coming down.
The hymns and requiems. The sense of movement
as you're borne along to the next place.

The Juggler At *Heaven's Gate*

For Michael Cimino

Behind the dirty table where Kristofferson is having
breakfast, there's a window that looks onto a nineteenth-
century street in Sweetwater, Wyoming. A juggler
is at work out there, wearing a top hat and a frock coat,
a little reed of a fellow keeping three sticks
in the air. Think about this for a minute.
This juggler. This amazing act of the mind and hands.
A man who juggles for a living.
Everyone in his time has known a star,
or a gunfighter. Somebody, anyway,
    who pushes somebody
around. But a juggler! Blue smoke hangs inside
this awful cafe, and over that dirty table where two
grownup men talk about a woman's future.
    And something,
something about the Cattlemen's Association.
But the eye keeps going back to that juggler.
That tiny spectacle. At this minute, Ella's plight
or the fate of the emigrants
is not nearly so important as this juggler's exploits.
How'd *he* get into the act, anyway? What's his story?
That's the story I want to know. Anybody
can wear a gun and swagger around. Or fall in love

144

with somebody who loves somebody else. But to *juggle*
for God's sake! To give your life to that.
To go with that. Juggling.

LONNY KANEKO

Earthquake Country

This poem began when I was born
and continued the next year when you
were born, and found a country full
of earthquakes shaking down our forty years.
Tule Lake, ice, dust, a range of mountains,
barbed wire, Minidoka kept us apart.
In Tule, neighbors pointed their fingers:
"Inu! Inu!" Knives flashed.
From Minidoka, a far fire lit
the western horizon.

After the war they shipped us back
like boy scouts from camp, assuming the doors
of our houses stood swinging open,
that lettuce and beans still filled the fields,
that customers stood waiting for our stores to open.
That long summer at camp became a long winter
full of a hundred faults. Your father raised
apples, deer, chicken, and weeds for other men
until he died for what the war had shaken loose.
My father cut grass for 15 years,
waiting for the world to shake loose a miracle
20 years long, full of dying chickens.

When your father died, you lost
your mother; one boy friend after another
tumbled through your life and faded

like childhood. "We will be here,"
you said, "after all this has gone,
like two sparrows in a tree, waiting for dawn."
You survive your marriage the way
you survived your father's death.

My marriage began in a newlywed world of basement
apartment dwellers who own their own world
but not the floors above, who are flooded
with dripping faucets, flushing toilets,
pot roasts being damned back to dust
and screaming (one day a platter flew
through their window, grew wings,
and wafted down in pieces).

Once I was trapped in a second story
wood framed flat halfway to the bath,
stretched taut as a garter
between door and floor, caught
between necessities of flesh and gravity.
Like all rubbery beings, master or mastered,
stretched or broken or snapping together,
I straightened on loose legs
in a bouncing bed-braced adolescent world
of shakey geometry and learned, too late,
the amplitude of shock
can flatten me.

I am alone now, the way you were alone,
divorce islands me from my children.
Your marriage is a continent between us.
Seattle fog and multiple sclerosis
can split us down the middle
but we survive them all
not knowing where the next quake will be.

In this country there are no chairs
to crawl under, no doorways to brace our lives.
No use heading for a bamboo grove where none exists
or hitting the dirt in the open field
and trying to hold the ground together.

We keep our balance,
feeling for the wave.
We ride it out,
our toes hanging over
the shifting plates of earth.

PART THREE

The Explanation

"So I return to the world I know, the heron as it pumps singly away from the marsh at dusk, the mixes of neon outside taverns calling to souls, the urging, the unknowing, a hundred million suns above the fall farmland"

James Grabill

ARTHUR SZE

Evil Grigri

Evil grigri:
taste acid in the word *sybaritic*.
Feel deer antlers polished in rain and sun;
taste green almonds,
the polar ice cap of Mars melting at the tip
    of your tongue.

Is it possible to wake
dressed in a tuxedo smoking a cigarette
    staring at a firing squad?
A man is cursed
when he remembers he cannot remember his dream;
taste sugar in the word *voluptuous;*
feel a macaw feather brush across your closed eyelids.

See the dead laugh at the pile of shoes at Dachau.
See as a man with one eye
the dead alive and singing,
walking down the equinoctial axis of the midnight street.

Now feel how the ocarina of your body
waits for pleasure to blow and make an emerald sound
    in the air;
make an apotropaic prayer
that the day's evil become the day's wild thyme:

say guava-passionflower-hibiscus salt,
say sun-sea wave,
say wind-star, venom-night,
say mango-river, eucalyptus-scented fang.

The Aphrodisiac

"Power is my aphrodisiac."
Power enables him to
connect a candle-lit dinner
to the landing on the moon.

151

He sees a plot in the acid
content of American soil,
malice in a configuration
of palm leaf shadows.
He is obsessed with
the appearance of democracy
in a terrorized nation.
If the price of oil
is an owl claw, a nuclear
reactor is a rattlesnake
fang. He has no use
for the song of an oriole,
bright yellow wings.
He refuses to consider
a woman in a wheelchair
touching the shadow of
a sparrow, a campesino
dreaming of spring.
He revels in the instant
before a grenade explodes.

The Negative

A man hauling coal in the street is stilled forever.
Inside a temple, instead of light

a slow shutter lets the darkness in.
I see a rat turn a corner running from a man with a chair
    trying to smash it,

see people sleeping at midnight in a Wuhan street on
    bamboo beds,
a dead pig floating, bloated, on water.

I see a photograph of a son smiling who two years ago
    fell off a cliff
and his photograph is in each room of the apartment.

I meet a woman who had smallpox as a child, was
    abandoned by her mother
but who lived, now has two daughters, a son, a son-in-law;

they live in three rooms and watch a color television.
I see a man in blue work clothes whose father
    was a peasant

who joined the Communist party early but by the time of
    the Cultural Revolution
had risen in rank and become a target of the Red Guards.

I see a woman who tried to kill herself with an
    acupuncture needle
but instead hit a vital point and cured her chronic asthma.

A Chinese poet argues that the fundamental difference
    between East and West
is that in the East an individual does not believe himself

in control of his fate but yields to it.
As a negative reverses light and dark

these words are prose accounts of personal tragedy
    becoming metaphor,
an emulsion of silver salts sensitive to light,

laughter in the underground bomb shelter converted into
    a movie theater,
lovers in the Summer Palace park.

LINDA HOGAN

The Truth Is

In my left pocket a Chickasaw hand
rests on the bone of the pelvis.
In my right pocket
a white hand. Don't worry. It's mine
and not some thief's.
It belongs to a woman who sleeps in a twin bed
even though she falls in love too easily,

153

and walks along with hands
in her own empty pockets
even though she has put them in others
for love not money.

About the hands, I'd like to say
I am a tree, grafted branches
bearing two kinds of fruit,
apricots maybe and pit cherries.
It's not that way. The truth is
we are crowded together
and knock against each other at night.
We want amnesty.

Linda, girl, I keep telling you
this is nonsense
about who loved who
and who killed who.

Here I am, taped together
like some old civilian conservation corps
passed by from the great depression
and my pockets are empty.
It's just as well since they are masks
for the soul, and since coins and keys
both have the sharp teeth of property.

Girl, I say,
it is dangerous to be a woman of two countries.
You've got your hands in the dark
of two empty pockets. Even though
you walk and whistle like you aren't afraid
you know which pocket the enemy lives in
and you remember how to fight
so you better keep right on walking.
And you remember who killed who.
For this you want amnesty
and there's that knocking on the door
in the middle of the night.

Relax, there are other things to think about.
Shoes for instance.
Now those are the true masks of the soul.

154

The left shoe
and the right one with its white foot.

Small Animals at Night

Surprised in sleeping flesh
they wake up
the boundaries of sleep.

The crow settles wings
in with the hands
and quiet cattle have gone their way.

Compadre, I say to the stray dog.
Nino, the bridled raven
waiting for night
with dancing feet
and fingerbones about its neck
like the ones men fashioned
from the hands of slaves.

Even the air is a judas goat
air that flies birds
in from the sky,
air snakes glide beneath
with eyes, red diamonds,
and the moon at their backs
drifting like sand.

Dark hills move
through wire and highways
and the soft black leaves
that slip through our eyes
to trees growing at the edge of the world.

Citizens move about,
a does curls in
spine against spine.
Silent,
but hear them.

155

They sing in their own heads
in the shivering blue bones of an ear
the voices here in grace
in the hollows of this body.

All Winter

In winter I remember
how the white snow
swallowed those who came before me.
They sing from the earth.
This is what happened to the voices.
They have gone underground.

I remember how the man named Fire
carried a gun. I saw him
burning.
His ancestors live in the woodstove
and cry at night and are broken.
This is what happens to fire.
It consumes itself.

In the coldest weather, I recall
that I am in every creature
and they are in me.
My bones feel their terrible ache
and want to fall open
in fields of vanished mice
and horseless hooves.

And I know how long it takes
to travel the sky,
for buffalo are still living
across the drifting face of the moon.

These nights the air is full of spirits.
They breathe on the windows.
They are the ones that leave fingerprints
on glass when they point out
the things that happen,
the things we might forget.

156

SAM HAMILL

In The Company Of Men

At the northern edge of this country
where the rain halts only
to be snow, the great glaciers wander
the slow indifferent centuries
toward the sea. Perched high
in frozen evergreens, real eagles
scan the bays below. No rag
wavering in the wind can set their hearts
to beat, no printed illustration
conveys the anger of their eyes,
nor the serious ease
only animals can attain. I walk
late morning sunrise near the bay.
The gray dawn breaks over peaks
of gray as I listen to the gulls—
they bicker and squabble
over scraps thrown out from
wintered trawlers.
                          Yesterday,
having paid my final visit
to the inmates, Lemon Creek Prison,
the heavy doors banged finally closed
behind me, and I remembered again
the same doors from twenty-five
years before when I was still
a boy, and something sank
so far in me that I could not speak
its name. Not fear, but the leaden
hand of day-to-day despair
like a metal fist
clutching the heart
unmercifully. We, all of us,
are guilty. Yet the few endure

the great indignities
we all must share.
                    The scraps
I toss away are words, no more.
I want to offer hope, a hand
of brotherhood across the steely dark
to pay my share of the fee
for the pound of human flesh
that faceless angel of revenge demands.
I take away their faces carved
into my mind with razor blades: Allen,
who speaks Chinese and knows
the strength within; Tom's serious
eyes and undeveloped gift
for muscular description; Reggie,
who looked a thousand miles in me
the time I mentioned Malcolm.
Gray rain slanting narrow streets
can't blur the echo of strong voices.
The cold from which I shiver
is the cold of self, within. I walk alone
but am in the company of men,
and as I move a little closer to
the stone that marks what a life had been,
something in me cries, *Begin.*
Although I leave alone
as each of us
must do, we, all of us
together, are going slowly home.

Getting it Wrong Again

". . . civilizations are as short-lived as weeks of our
    lives. . . ."
and slowly, in the middle,
                    I close the book and lay aside
the unreal world.
                    Clouds continue to gather
overhead, outside, sliding in from the sea.

                     Nothing distinguishes them,
one from the other, but bulk or weight
                   or the pathetic tint
gray sunlight lends their hair.
              Thus the universal
devours each particular, each life
            reduced to its essential. What
can I know
     is not a question. Of course, I wanted power, I wanted
the power to save,
           not a civilization, but one small petal
from its blossom.
        For in its perfect hour
it was lovely. But not a week. Not even
          one whole day—this perfect
product of ten thousand
         thousand years—perfection—
before the cleansing rain.
        Before the hand
protects the heart with its tight fist again.

JIM SIMMERMAN

The Dead Madonnas Of Santiago

What words have I for the dead
madonnas of Santiago,
their eyes like smoke in rainfall?
On Palm Sunday they stir
in that half hour,
half-breath
when the moon is a chalice
of blood
tipped to the world's lip.
By torchglow

they follow narrow paths
out of the mountains,
their earrings flashing,
their full hips swaying like wheat
before a storm.
They wind into the hushed
streets of the village,
a procession
of murmurs:
Christe eleison.

Once a year they come like this,
like banished lepers,
to dip from the cool waters
of the living,
to fill the heavy stone jars
we leave by the well.
They bear them upon their heads
back into the mountains,
to their children
who wait
with the thirst of the dead.
And if, laboring
beneath the weight of her gift,
one stumbles,
soaking her long braids,
her skirt,
puddling the parched earth,
what has been lost
is nothing,
is not a drop.

Ricky Ricardo Drinks Alone

I-yi-yi-yi! look at that moon
floating up there like a teaspoon
of sweet cane sugar or the head
of a conga drum. Someone said

160

the man in the moon is an old
Cuban fisherman who sold
his boat for enough bay rum
to sail out of his body one
soft Havana night, and half
the time I think it's true. Laugh
if you like, but I have watched
his eyes fix upon the thatched
hat of a woman who waits
each night by the dock for her late
sailor to return, only to
see the morning paint a blue
and emptier harbor, only to turn
once more from the sea and yearn
slowly home, across fallow
tideland. Her long yellow
dress made her look, from
a distance, like a canary, come
to sing the forests back.

        What
has become of the rain that cut
through the night like maracas? And
of the flower monger whose hand
was a warm garden on my neck? And of
the sails that hovered like doves
on the horizon? And of the clop-
clop-clop of Lucinda? I want to stop
the moon with a bray sometimes. I
want to bray so sweetly it will fly
backward, like an empty bottle
over my shoulder. Bray until
I am back on the beach with my
father, learning to tie
a bowline, mend a net. There
was a song he sang—I remember
how the surf beat out time, though
the words, the words . . . Low
tide left me shells shaped like
pink fans. Luck was the bright
bit of glass I found one day. Keep it

close, he told me. Memory is a ship
in a bottle. The bottle breaks.

Then Again

suppose the soul is a stone
and not the holy cellophane
I've fancied it,
and thus—like the body
shorn of heat, stripped
even of the heart's
flimsy flam—
does not hover, waft, ascend,
breaststroke its way
into a panoramic hereafter
(flourish of French horns
and the multitudes joined
in a sheepish rendition
of the Twenty-third Psalm).
Yes, I think the soul
is a stone and sticks
with the body,
frazzled compadre.
And that is why we shut
the dead behind doors
without knobs
and chuck them in holes
and snub them.
That is why we leave
pages of marble
or even small houses
atop them—
to press them smooth,
to weigh them on their way.
It is the soul
steers the body,
scuttles it so
it won't be recovered

by the sharpest shovel,
the deepest sigh. . . .
And heaven is a dark place
hidden somewhere
in the earth's hard gut
where a few stones,
the lucky ones,
roll together finally
and are still.
And that is why I keep
always a few pebbles
buried in my pockets.
You could call it
honoring the dead.
I call it getting started.

NANCY ANDREWS

There, Where The Ground Swells

It came with pure cadence
strict as Latin, strong as ten Northern Oaks
inevitable as the rings that grow
however slowly at their centers . .

cool lake of long glass without reflection
chalk line of solitude
stone
this silent architecture—a module
of my mother's death.

But I am among many energies—wind of her fire
opaque spirit
among layers of many crossings—intersectings . .
as birds dart
as drops of water intersect the sun

springing from the fountain
resonant as metal—incandescent.

There, where the ground swells,
the throated earth,
lies her determination
among swollen roses.

I hear her,
the birds singing texts of triangles
through the morning breeze and wide acres.
Here,
stenciled on the perfect side
the perfect Nature of it,
is a morning of fresh speaking.

Death must be when the sky is invisible

but I see the sky—reach out my sight
looking for her
and sense filaments, in the blue light.

Mine Shaft

Better understand
that life here is metal
determined women, hard at the elbow
who know the tooth of the mountain
lights the surface
of their man's brain. .

pulls them underneath
like dark lions.
Something almighty heavy
from the long line of their fathers
takes them there
or maybe the incessant flicker of fools gold
trapped in a corner of their minds.

The women see from various windows
the tailings pond—testimony

to the strand of hair
that falls in their eyes. .
they should get something
from the counters they polish
like silver slivers, gold dust—something unreal
a cerulean surface
like a nice day at the end of the tunnel
that they slant toward.

ALBERTO RIOS

What a Lemon Teaches

Lemons. I like them. Light, and green,
Gardener's green, golfball shapes.
In summer, some days, I sip them
Tenderly through, take their insides
Into my idle, my ice-numb mouth,
Their meat amusing, making my face
Fall to the floor, or farther still,
My sugar saved, for sucking, or for horses.

Lemons. I lick them, like the bitter
Biting of their borders, whose breath suggests
A jumping, aging, juxtapositions, folded
fists, fire's phlegm as it lingers.

Limón. Mamá, ¡que amarga la limonada!
Another name names me.
My mother's mother, *mamá*, speaks
Her special sounds, secret in my ear:
I hear bees, ease my way
Toward the woman, and wait for more.
I move my mouth, mimicking hers:
How heavy, how full

It feels, and afraid: of failing, of not
Having knelt enough, not like her legs.

Lemons. I live them, *el limón,*
The meat, my mother's mother's scream:
The sour skin—her sweat—for what
One winter wildly would be
A baby. A boy. Alberto. Albertito.
You take your time tonight, she says.
Be sad. Suffer. Shake in your bed.

Be brave in biting lemons.
Love to take a long, a long time.
Tomorrow, tomorrow, tomorrow remember
This moment; me; remember how
I hold your hand, and Hurt you, you
So young: allá, the yellow lemons,
Like them less. Love me.
Make me the marrow in your bones.

I bite. It's bitter. I break a skin
Of celebration, suck the seeds, and spit.

City of Knives

Across the Line
Was Mexico, it was
A dare.
The men
Were all around us:
Girls' fathers
Who taught them not to let us,
Brothers who yelled
you broke the salt shaker,
Friends who gave us things
We thought were free.
A man, being a man: it was
To take
The five-finger discount
In the Kress 5&nothing,

To go inside white Julie
Behind the thick oleanders,
To take it all
And give nothing,
Give a knife
To the side of a face.

Canal Street
We talked about
You more than anything
In the lockerroom,
This man's kitchen.
Canal Street, the red
And the old green
Neon of the *over there,*
Of the La Conga
With its mache palms
And the open legs
Of the whistling women
There, at the top of the stairs
Where we could almost see
Into the curling black
Of the red, very red dresses.

To spit in the eyes
Of the men daring us—
The men were everywhere—
One of our zippers finally
Went down
To speak for us all,
to prove,
On the steps of the football field
And we watched an arm
Come out of those jeans later
Lit up and red
from doing it, don't you know anything?
Lit up, red,
More beautiful that moment
Than the face
Of any woman.

Mason Jars by the Window

Yes, but beyond happiness what is there?
The question has not yet been answered.
No great quotations have issued forth
From there, we have no still photographs
Full of men in fine leather hiking boots,
Women with new-cut walking sticks.
              So yes, it is the realm of thin tigers
Prowling, out to earn even more stripes;
It is the smell of seven or eight perfumes
Not currently available in America.
              Maybe this is wrong, of course.
The place may after all be populated,
Or over-populated, with dented trash cans
In the streets and news of genital herpes
In every smart article in every slick magazine
Everywhere in the place.
              But everybody there smiles—
Laughs, even, every time a breath can be caught.
This is all true.
Beyond happiness, it's all the same,
Things come back to where we are now.
Of course maybe this is wrong,
But don't believe it: a happiness exists,
All right, I have seen it for myself,
Touched it, touched the woman
Who with her daughter together keep
Ammonia in Mason jars by the side window.
They will throw it all in his face God
Damn him if he ever comes close again.

PAMELA USCHUK

What You May Have Thought Was Empty

Perhaps no one was home
so you went quiet as air behind a leaf
for a walk in the arroyo
swaying with the sun's dry current.
You were restless,
looking for a place to sit and watch
your shadow stain the ground.
Or
while your feet rearranged broken feldspar
like angry words, you saw
a black beetle big as your ear
even with its head broken off.
You stopped, thinking it moved.
But it was empty,
a stranded desert nautilus.
So, with your skin pricked by rose quartz,
you sat while mica gleamed
like constellations around your feet, around
the beetle who was a shell,
and you dreamed it had been left for you.
You walked inside the beetle
as you would a cave,
prospecting for the ganglia,
the missing heart.
When you awoke, you didn't wonder
that you picked up the shell
and brought it home.
Maybe you were thinking about your lover
or your children
or what to have for lunch, and instead
of answering the phone
that rang distant as a vireo's call,
you sat at the table
placing the beetle on your plate.

For a moment you imagined eating it
so that black indifferent shell
would fill you but you could see,
inside the thorax
you thought was empty, a tiny light
like the flash of animal eyes
struck by headlights on a lonely road,
and your hand opened.

After Reading Louise Bogan's Journals

Outside on this floodplain
subdivision, the hiss and pant
of irrigation hoses
disturbs air day and night.
Theirs is an awful breathing,
the monotonous whisper of locusts.
Relentless witness,
ubiquitous desire, it is
the sound of water that soothes and erodes.

What peril life places us in
when love fails
the heart. The heart,
the watershed of the mind.
What peril when the flume
claims us and we become
the woman whose hand rakes
the parlor wall to stop the flowing
as we sink in water so transparent
we see no arm above ours,
no lips saying no.

There rises in each of us
a mad woman as afraid
of water as of losing love.
She cries when we walk into surf,
wounds us as we lie
beside rivers

whose currents could cleanse our tears.
She is what
we always hear listening to the sad frenzy
of tides. What could drown us
we drink to live.

I won't say I know
how it was for you, just as I
can't reproduce in my garden
the exact red-rimmed yellow eye
of the marigold that silenced all the roses
in your mother's hospital room.
It grew indelible in your young eyes
just as the crash of the mill flume
circled your ear each time love fled.

Later, during breakdowns, you refused
the awful anxiety of roses,
their red petals
fussy drawing rooms you couldn't enter.
Water was aluminum in the painful pitcher
beside your bed, keeping you awake
with its thin waves washed
against unyielding shores.
Giving up on fickle lovers,
the husband who broke your dreams,
you gave yourself to words
that emptied around you when the last attack came.
They echo still.
I would have told you then
water would carry you, that finally
water forgives the heart.

JANE KOPP

Farm Wife

the earth so hard
no nail could be driven in
above whitened grass
air dims

too hot to weep
and no use
but her cheekbones ache
lying across the bed

through rusty screen wire
blackberries die
okra and
the very trees
drop leaves

two days ago
in the afternoon
a light rain
fell
minutes on end

all that wealth of dust
was briefly fragrant

Dirt Road

Braked, on a promontory of red earth,
The automobile hangs pendulous, ticking in heat
Upon the throb of insects in the arroyo;
And the dust subsides behind it that was raised
Reaching this spot, which is dry and bare,
So that the car seems to have arrived
In a new place and nowhere.

                         I am flotsam
In jetsam, here with broken beer bottles
And the nested, circular smash of something
large, of clearer glass; here with orange
Weedblooms, on the slope near a pinon tree,
Straying from the shadow at the trunk
Into the glare. Though lower down,
In the lower atmosphere in which blue consumes,
Telephone wires dip motionless against the hills,
The long shadows projected by their poles
Draining away to the right on the leached-out slope,
Here, in enormous silence, I am miles
From any code to transmit or receive;
The long wires charged with language pass me by.
Everything here is banal, random and free
And teases the mind with odd and radical meanings
About to coalesce in some new way:

In moments like this, rarely, boredom nears
The naught of contemplation; the vast, tired
Skin of things feels a wind of unknown source
And stirs, about to bell in a larger round
Or rise to some new, sweeter altitude
(Mystics make landfalls on the
Shore of a main lacuna never yet mapped).

Almost round on top, the distant hill
Meets, cool and solid, the impingement of hot sky.
Nearer, in the ash of an old fire
Scattered like tea leaves, a solitary ant
Nervously investigates a group
Of many, small, peculiarly shaped red stones.

MICHAEL SIMMS

The Blue Heron

Beside the road leading here
I saw the bonehouse of a dead quail, askew
in its wings. Drunk
and lost in west Hell I'd stopped
in a taxidermist's shop
for directions. The only living thing there
pointed down the road
then tried to sell me you.

Rigid on a wire stand beside a stuffed fox
with a surprised look in his glass eye,
your ponderous wings extended,
your dorsal feathers too high,
your long legs dangling behind you like a rudder,
your minuscule head cocked,
you were locked in flight forever
ridiculous, grotesque.

But now, you stand on the cold shore, you sway.
Your cry starts low in your throat, rises
as you throw your head back, glides down the scale
as your head descends, the pitch
slipping upward with a lilt at the end.

Behind you, clouds gather above the promontory.
The light is like a great beached whale.
Seagulls slide by. Crows.
The seagulls blue in the blue levels of dawn.
The crows blue.
You stand in the salt shallows,
gaunt, motionless, quiet
where the tide washes minnows in.
A glimmer and you spear it, flip
the fish over and swallow it, headfirst.

The Explanation

I think there is a likeness to all things.
The woods always seem to be waiting
for us to move on, so the trees
may resume their patient chemistry.

A painter friend tells me
he can't paint a tree
except by becoming one,
learning the activities of light.

I could study for years and never learn
what love teaches in a day.
My stepson shoots marbles.
His mind opens the fable:
what occurs once, occurs often.

The moon rises
in the transparent darkness, the air
filling with birds, the smell of pine and hay
and Christopher chants a line
measured by a poet fifty years before:
the moon, the moon is at the door.

WALTER PAVLICH

On Not Growing Up With Fireflies

Fireflies ascend the rain-coming air,
each arc governed by the need
for another light like its own.
They give up feeding
and just swallow air
or the flight-scent of a luminous mate.
I missed them as a boy

175

too many clouds spilling
over to douse them.

But even then I knew
my eyes would not save me
for what I wanted to see.
I used a cracker-hole
to pierce the world—
crows hooked on a telephone pole,
water lifting out of the sea.

I can view them now
in the amphitheatre of the midwest
bits of dry lightning
cruising and resting.
Bewildered moths veer toward
their intermittent illumination.
I have faith in these aviators
on fire with their on again
off again nocturnal ignition,
these quick sparks of eternity.

The Albino Raccoon, Folsom City Zoo

—for the staff and volunteers of the Folsom Zoo

I would give you
   your own stream,
my rare milk-eyed one,
   for crayfish dipping
into the blind water,
   their leavings unreflected
in each lost iris,
   and sky swept clean of hawks.
Victim of color,
   your beauty outlined
by sadness with no dark
   dark enough to rest in.
So this cage.

At first, I thought,
opossum, with the tail rings
   dropped off,
face-mask abandoned.
   Somehow you found
the one corner
   of caged sun,
and let loose
   your winter shudder,
dozing until my shadow
   became just another presence
with nothing to offer,
   your nose pinching
the air brittle
   between us.
My gentle survivor,
   hopeless in any world,
you cannot see
   or know how many others
hide themselves,
   thinking they're not obvious,
Just like you.

With Eleanor Near the End of a Minus Tide

The moon has allowed
us this walk
under the oblong circuits
of guillemots, their tucked feet
giving red dashes to the sky,
near the cormorant skeins
netting the jumpy tide.
We climb oceanside
around the brown amplitude
of Haystack Rock,
mother and son managing
dank avenues water has made.
We're barnacles long floating apart

177

attached to each other's hands.
My shoe rides the slime-slide
of an iridescent seaweed blade
and my knee opens up fresh
colors like a sudden childhood memory.
You dab it with your dead mother's
handkerchief, washing it
with dips out of a tidepool bowl.
Gulls let loose white
like liquid rocks smacking
around us. You've been 48 years
with the same man
but for the first time touch
the heart of an anemone.
Tentacles fold over your fingers
their tips lace patterns of old rose
sticky as a moviehouse floor
tugging your skin.
Now you are not surprised
it is an animal.
Because you never taught me
these things, we are teaching
each other. Huddles of sea stars
tighten their hold on the afternoon.
There are not enough minutes
for you to close each anemone.
Highwater begins
brushing the sea palms.
We cannot lie down
with a quilt of stone
and purple sponge.
We've just time
to help each other
back towards sand
and remember during sleep
where we were
and where the water will be.

MELINDA MUELLER

A Teacher After the War

On one wall of the gallery hangs a still-life
of fruit and a fish slumped
with its pale belly reflected in a pewter bowl.
Across the room, by the same painter,
a nude reclines on drapery:
the curve of her hip and plump
white thigh glimmer like the belly of the fish.
Perhaps the artist was amused
by the resemblance. Or else the smiling nude
is a portrait of his grief.
In either case, out of irony or pain
two paintings, his work. And this gallery
the work of an architect; outside,
the engineers' streets and bridges—All the made,
labored-over properties of this world.
And what is my work? I've said sometimes,
"I love my work," and meant
my students, but I don't create them. Every year
they are the same age, while I get older.
This is the gift that teaching gives
a teacher: to see your life lived over
and over till you understand. They think
themselves clumsy, and in their young dismay
they move in a quandary of grace.
Once I was so dismayed. My own growing up's reshaped
in watching them, the memories of it haunted less
by fear of failure. I was, for one thing, able
to give solace, since I was once like them. And they . . .
I used to think, seeing those old photographs
of the Union and Confederate dead: *Bare ruined choirs.*
This one who was quick of mind, this
who knew Keats by heart
or could write an elegant proof. Where is my work—
what soured ground in Asia is its issue?

179

Let artists paint fuel for bonfires, then.
Let us landscape avenues
for the sake of rubble afterwards. I loved
my work, that the world has made short work of.

Driving Past Commercial Tulip Fields

Hills tip up around the edges of the flood plain,
which the road's neat gray triangle bisects

(we've driven toward the sharp apex all afternoon).
This time of day, light gets ventriloquial,

having less to do with the sun than with that silvered barn;
or perhaps it's an exhalation from the vivid fields.

In all these miles of red, purple, white, and yellow
tulips, could we find the one enflamed

with messianic fervor? It's just the light,
or a cartoonist's fancy: tulips with their two leaves

upraised, and each soldierly stem topped
by a large cephalic blossom. Nonetheless,

with this suggestion of something hidden and intended,
the slagheaps of mown tulips—Darwins,

Rembrandts, Mendels, Archbishops, Emperors—
that fill the ditches by the road become

disturbing. Behind the hills to the west
billows the ocean, whose wet breath

sustains the crowded fields. The boom
of one breaker is swallowed by boom of the next,

pounding on the breastbone like the hollow thud
of fear. On the massive basalt stacks offshore,

cormorants stretch out their soaked wings to dry, black
and cruciform in silhouette. It's dusk, and one,

alarmed by something in the disembodying
mist, cries out three times hoarsely, cries

180

that don't seem impersonal. No: it's not
what we sometimes think, that the world can be

quite human, but that the world's so old
it's tried everything already, and more than once:

grace, abandonment, the thing made once and never
made again, the heretical notion of individual survival.

STANLEY NOYES

The Dream Painter

He paints sheep of the Sierras, or elsewhere,
each ewe and lamb in the flock
el rebano, in its blue meadow
but whiter, cleaner than in life, as if

each ram had been scrubbed, valued
as a unique shape, plain sheep
as if each had importance, and next
sketches in the shepard, *el pastor,*
brushes in his dark-blue shoulder

in watercolor but leaves incomplete
the hand that dangles, white, in pencil
lines, that hand which later will draw
the knife along the throat of the lamb.

The Book And The City

In a night silver as frost the traveler
roams a town of adobe hovels,
descends an alley between shanties
while clouds blacken the moon

181

and he passes the near-ruin of a shack
with rusted washtub dumped before it—

but halts suddenly at the soft
edge of an arroyo where water rustles,
spinning to confront a man dressed
in a business suit, who, for a second,
lays a hand on his chest, as if
to shove him backward off the brink;

he grabs the stranger's jacket,
threatening to drag him along. For a minute,
under a strangled moon, it's a standoff,
until the traveler utters his name,
thrusts out a hand, which the other grips,
at which the stranger, a salesman, also

itinerant, gives him an ancient dictionary:
as clouds recede, the salesman demands
to know if the traveler travels in time.
The traveler does not answer,
noticing the stranger's face is similar
to his own as a young man, but climbs

the alley to trash and the shanty, reads
its shattered windows by moonlight, black
shrieks beyond his hearing,
yet recognizes the place as his,
its door the one to turn into, where
by the book in his hand, he'll rebuild the city.

JAMES GRABILL

An Earthen Night

Oxygen drinks down into the flames
of the houses and rooms set back
in electric lights with people talking.

The cool night drinks down after work
into hard floors and sheets of TV light
through the sound of ice in the glasses.

Oxygen of the fields buried in streets
drinks down, into cooling engines, back
from new speeds and ultraviolet clouds

of birth pulsing invisibly from red hospitals,
tender meat smells swelling over the river
and drinking down railroads with thoughts

where cups pile up, and strangers carrying
part of us disguised at the door,
and identity buried in hotel lobbies

and duties that have been waiting
for us to come here, broken into headlights
shining back, toward the turning over

of last century, with a few gulls
over crystal vaults of big buildings,
distant white whales diving through

blue lights in the water, listening
to pouring walls of fish in their waves,
squids shooting out into black flocks

of water, sand crabs on dunes
in the waves of breath, like bears
sleeping, pain breaking off bodies

forgetting where they began, the night
drinking down the horns of each worm,
down the tiny breastbones of spiders

and fish masks echoing, cat bones
where ice forms, where a brother walks
with the negligee of dusk gliding

ahead of him, the green wheat rising
behind him with insect spines
darting, in the human shaded sound

of our voices, and the cool night
drinking down the spiral halls
of plants and the sax bellowing.

A Fall

So I return to the world I know, the heron
as it pumps singly away from the marsh at dusk,
the mixes of neon outside taverns calling to souls,
the urging, unknowing, a hundred million suns
above the fall farmland, bread light of streets
after 10 p.m., the drafty buses speeding past
houses where people we will never see are home,
symphonies like ocean volumes going unheard
in the whale city, symphonies stretched in time,
the rock unhooking a story, western song
lost in struggle between man and woman, city
and natural decay of what has fallen.
                                        I return
to the forms of life as they power the neighborhoods,
growing on earth, bearing children. The meadows
of the tables converse with Bach apartment windows.
Hands of the workers move in the grace of light
that comes through tinted glass. The callings of herds
blanket the minute hand. The train shudders,
its memory of a thawing river, the avalanche
of her blouse.
                    I return the snakes of that car
to the host. I return the willful curtain of form
to the beating of a dog's heart. I return the red nails
to the tub beans and her glance to the gaze of Genesha
in the centuries of stone carving. I return
these lifetimes of smoke.
                              I turn back the covers
on the bed. The owl wakes beneath skirts of pine
needles. Behind the house, there is another cliff,
the columns of numbers, mansions of tides,
of understandings, where few go after dark, where
urging longs in the scent of earth, the foliage,
solar systems of unformed things, informed
elements, the planets seen between distant suns
above the neighborhood.

We need the earthen cities
that fly over the roof at night, fish moving
invisibly in waves of a hand, and after a rain
the massive golden leaves around a person's body,
turn of an apple edge beneath bending derricks
and tavern salts, abandon of each shape we took,
in light from the roots of ferns. We know
we will live in each other until we die.

TESS GALLAGHER

The Kneeling One

I was taking the little needed, not more,
so the earth could carry me, the way
a tree is able for many birds at once if
they are sure to leave and bear themselves
lightly. I was thinking of home, wanting to
go there again, stepping along the roadside
with a branch I had chosen. Came
horses. Came men
on the horses. Their faces
pressed to my neck.

After, I was changed and did not know
how to show it. When they were gone
I started for home. One horse
they left for me, red horse in sunlight,
brown horse in shadow. I knelt
to the horse. I led it beside me.
Where it grazed I slept.

One knee in homage, two in worship—
I worshipped, I paid homage. With

my two lips and my eyes did I kneel.
With my forehead and heart. I did so.
Perhaps at first it was simple entreaty
as among unsophisticated peoples who
wish only to be spared. But gradually,
as I knelt before a tree or river,
I saw it was more, more even than
reverence, this attention
that grew in me.

My knees became callus like a camel's.
My knees did ache and toughen. Not
like the Carthusians who, bending
the knee, would not touch earth, did I
kneel, but as Stephen knelt
before his death with those who had
stoned him looking on, knelt on
both knees and, I think, not
in prayer.

All manner of things and beings were
placed in my path—the hooves
of a slain deer, head of a murderer
fresh from the block, a basket of pears.
I am a spirit with many duties and no
masters, I said. I am the kneeling
one, and I knelt to each.
But what do you want? they asked.
It's not out of wanting, I said,
and passed on.

I reached home. I knelt to
the mother, to the womb that had borne
me. At my father's grave I stayed
kneeling as the dusk came down. He
did not speak, but he felt my kneeling,
of this I am certain. It made
a small bright ripple on the minds
of the dead.

A few onlookers followed me
in the blue twilight. Where will you

go now? they wanted to know.
I will go to the house of my childhood,
I said, and there I will kneel
and kneel down for a while.

GENE FRUMPKIN

Before the Meeting in the World Below

Palinurus, held in the hand of a solemn wit,
you fell headlong from your helm
into brine and blame. Too much belief
in a calm world, Aeneas said of you,
sailor. Not knowing how strong sleep is,
like a god. That sleep is the crystalline beam
centered in the mind's temple, cicerone
for all those who go, no matter how wary,
into the shade of a new map. Only
the author knew with what courage
you resisted, Palinurus, the somnolent
weavings of the stars, how clearly you saw
day being woven into false night. This author
who smiles, erasing your struggle
with a comic stroke of his pen, logged
one last boon of strength when, in falling,
you took with you—in life's deathly grip—
the lead ship's stern and steering oar.

The Metaphysics of Paper

Reading *The Confessions* of St. Augustine,
what most impressed me was the smell of humus.
Imbedded within the words, in each letter,

187

in each space between letters, was a wet sound,
not purely of water, wetness
that had impregnated woodpulp so the words
were heavy, rooted in some ancient tree
although the sound was aboveground. There was
in the saint's reflections a moist rigor.

As I listened, the words clung to air,
echoing the stolen pears from Tagaste
and a madrigal of vegetation from Oregon.
So what I read on my lips was more
than the bishop wrote. The paper itself
revealed a long walk in a remote forest
where sunlight seeped through the higher foliage
only to be absorbed in layers by the soil.
How to describe God's truth by such

underfooting of His unimaginable substance?
Confessions are for bedtime after a spare supper.
The crickets rub lazily then race to catch up
with destiny, now as I run my hand
over the glazed legend on the book's cover.
Once more the clouds, green with earthworms,
wander through my eyes, I smell the caul in them
and believe no story except what grows
dankly clear, creaturely on the tongue.

After Reading Some Poems by William Bronk

One languishes inside the local custom
of a world. As if tomorrow will come
without clothes, a tailor's dummy stuck with pins;
in a corner of the formless, some bolts of cloth.
Not that we lack source or spirit—
what we have is too much world.

One cuts into blue and snips out
the figure of a memory, a sky

on such-&-such a nameless day. We sew on
yellow eyes, a nose, a mouth, and so it's done,
that doll of sky. This is the real world,
the one that is in doubt. One gives it

a name, out of indifference or ennui,
or perhaps because identity is nothing more
than remembrance, a time buried in the tongue.
How to crush this habit! One travels elsewhere,
builds board by board a tiny house
under different stars, slips into fresh

habiliments, starts drinking papaya juice every night
before sleep. Dreams march through
at a brisker cadence, friendships grow like beets.
What was thought to be loneliness
now is seen as prolific solitude
dubbed with voices, with desired faces.

One listens and hears, finally, in the next room
loud shouting about some abstruse thread
that draws us together—fear, love, the minotaur.
Apprehending ourselves in the world *is* a world,
for the time, being. Whatever we say is required,
could not be other, not for the world.

FRANK STEWART

On The Pali Coast, Hawaii

for Michael Sykes

At dawn the lambs trot the fence perimeter.
At the gate I let them through
and with a dim wedge of silver glass
nailed to the post I shave in the mandarin light

that's slowly igniting the tips of the wild
grass. The wild *'ehako* are spinning overhead.
On the dark edge of the grove, the burrowing animals
are still out and busy in the brush.

In that light, feeling more like a lamb than a man,
like moisture on a boot or hat brim, I cross
to the higher fence through the crumbling basalt
and *pili* grass to check the locks
on the high range. I see the rams farther up
posture, halt, and glide away, then strike
defiant poses. The smell of the fresh stems and salt air
burns the chafed skin of my neck and clings
like burrs. The kiawe grove waves its fletchings.

Down the slopes, the deep-running fish
twirl in the green current. The blood in my heart
doubles, flops over and back, startled
at suddenly too much of everything.
Suddenly, something eternal.
"I will touch things, and no more thoughts,"
Jeffers said, in an upcountry like this one,
hearing too the jubilant rhythm
of dancing hooves and wings behind him
and the disobedient wildness.

Above June Lake

The seventh day we woke
cold weather had closed down like a grey wing
across the peaks, and only a pinfeather of blue
shone through the gap east toward Mono.
Snow had crusted our gear overnight—
and I rose, light as a bird in the mid-

delirious arms of pneumonia, awoke jubilant
at the gold-grey lake, the thin Sierra air.
The alders and stiff pines, the cliffs and talus
gleamed, it seemed to me, like silver candlesticks.

190

We'd never camped on high, Russ and me, two young
  boys—
had toted only spinning reels and light clothes. And
with a ranger's hand-drawn map we'd found the lake,
though a thousand feet higher than it should have been.
Down to nothing now but some canned fruit
and the fish we caught at dawn and dusk.

For me, body had become mind. And the fevered mind
was light and the clear cold things gold light made visible.
Russ grumbled, demanded we descend that afternoon,
for soon I was like the snow itself, unmanageable,
shimmering, ecstatic. We cast our spinners for a last

good meal. In the sizzling pan of mountain trout, we
spooned the last of the canned cherries, made coffee,
then buried what we couldn't carry down. The trek
was long and steep, but Russ insisted we press on—
worried I'd become intractable, though weak, hallucinating
   like some Spanish saint free from a lightless prison,
seeing sunlight for the first time, recognizing nothing.

Over the narrow ledge going down through what seemed
like daylight stars I began to fall, and felt
   the trees brush by
like feathers. I spread my arms, and
   like a redwing swooped
until the earth was small as a nest toward which I flew.

Overhead, a high flurry that could have been hawks,
some other creature of perfection.
The light closed down fast and I thought
how easy it is to have joy, how easy.

The Backwater Poets

for us all

Some look out and see only fire trails disappearing,
ragged forests, broken plains, a watery horizon.

Or flights of lonely mammals, the waterfowl
headed south, arctic plover on the summer trades.
And this Book of Nature almost speaks aloud:
"Your're a long ways from New York, aren't you,
   cowboy?"

Certainly there are no cities to speak of. Forget opera.
The Met, a decent Braque, a single Turner, a Bonnard.
But there are letters. Poems stuffed inside only a dozen
   others
will ever read, the description of an icy lake,
perhaps, ecstatic winter rain, a sad-eyed waitress
in Upper Michigan a poet could love, heartbreak
and darkness that link us better than print.

Only watercolor: forget ambition. Some lines
like deer holding for a moment in the headlights
before she dives away, a needle in the memory
miles later. And no commerce. No commerce. Just say
an accord, and a certain severity worn lightly.
Names writ in water—and bourbon, and red wine.

Contributors

PATRICIA GOEDICKE is the author of eight books of poetry, including *The Wind of Our Going* (Copper Canyon) and *Listen, Love* (Barnwood). She teaches in the writing program at the University of Montana in Missoula.

ROBERT BURLINGAME was educated at Brown University. His poems have appeared in numerous magazines and chapbooks, including *Eighteen Poems* (Poetry Texas) and *Tu Lu Yu in a Later Autumn* (Mesilla Press). He teaches literature at the University of Texas in El Paso.

LINDA BIERDS is the author of *Flights of the Harvest-Mare* (Ahsahta) and *Off the Aleutian Chain* (L'Epervier'). She has received fellowships from the Seattle Arts Commission and is an editor at the University of Washington.

KEITH WILSON is the author of twenty books of poetry, including *Stone Roses: Poems From Transylvania* (University of Utah) and *Retablos* (San Marcos). He lives in Las Cruces, New Mexico.

JOHN BRANDI is publisher of Tooth of Time Books in Santa Fe. His numerous books include *The Cowboy From Phantom Banks* (Floating Island) and *That Back Road In* (Wingbow).

WILLIAM PITT ROOT is the author of seven books of poetry, including *Faultdancing* (University of Pittsburgh). He has received grants from the Guggenheim and Rockefeller Foundations and has taught at various universities.

PAUL ZARZYSKI's two books of poetry are *Call Me Lucky* (Confluence) and *The Make-Up of Ice* (University of Georgia). He teaches in the writing program at the University of Montana in Missoula and is a champion rodeo bareback rider.

JODY ALIESAN's four books of poetry include *Doing Least Harm* (Brooding Heron) and *Desire* (Empty Bowl). She received an NEA fellowship in 1978 and lives on Waldron Island, Washington.

NAOMI SHIHAB NYE's three books of poetry are *Different Ways to Pray, Hugging the Jukebox,* and *Yellow Glove,* all from Breitenbush Books. She has received two Texas Institute of Letters Awards in poetry and lives in San Antonio, Texas.

DAVID ROMTVEDT is a graduate of the Iowa Writers' Workshop. His two books are *Moon* (Bieler Press), a poetry collection, and *Free and Compulsory for All* (Graywolf), short prose. He divides his time between Port Townsend, Washington and Buffalo, Wyoming.

JACK HEFLIN graduated from the writing program at the University of Montana in Missoula. His poems have appeared in *Cutbank, The Bloomsbury Review,* and other magazines. He teaches at a small college in Monroe, Louisiana.

GEORGE KALAMARAS is the publisher of Talking Leaves Press. His book of poetry is *Heart Without End* (Leaping Mountain Press). He teaches at Colorado State University in Fort Collins.

STEVE SANFIELD became the first Storyteller-In-Residence in the U.S., in 1977, under the sponsorship of the California Arts Council. His books include *A New Way* (Tooth of Time) and *A Natural Man-The True Story of John Henry* (Godine). He lives in Nevada City, California.

SANDRA ALCOSSER's book, *A Fish to Feed All Hunger* (University of Virginia) was the 1984 Associated Writing Program's winner in poetry. She has taught at Louisana State and San Diego State Universities and makes her home in the Bitterroot Mountains of Montana.

SUSAN TICHY's book of poetry, *The Hands in Exile* (Random House) was a winner in the 1983 National Poetry Series. She lives in Westcliffe, Colorado. Her second book of poetry, *A Smell of Burning Begins the Day,* is forthcoming from Wesleyan in 1988.

JOY HARJO was born in Oklahoma and is a member of the Creek Tribe. Her three books of poetry include *She Had Some Horses* (Thunder Mouth Press). She plays saxophone for the jazz band, Lip Service, and teaches at the University of Colorado in Boulder.

STEVEN WHITE is the author of two books of poetry and has edited and translated two anthologies of Latin American poetry for Unicorn Press: *Poets of Nicaragua 1916–1979* and *Poets of Chile 1965–1985.* He lives in Eugene, Oregon.

NANCY MAIRS' book of poetry, *In All the Rooms of the Yellow House* (Confluence) was awarded the Western States Book Award in poetry. She is also the author of *Plaintexts* (University of Arizona). She was a visiting lecturer at UCLA in 1986–87 and lives in Tucson, Arizona.

JIMMY SANTIAGO BACA's two books of poems are *What's Happening* (Curbstone Press) and *Poems Taken From My Yard* (Timberline). He lives on a farm south of Albuquerque, New Mexico where he raises cattle and sells fruit and alfalfa.

JOSEPH HUTCHISON is the author of *The Undersides of Leaves* (Wayland Press) and two Juniper Press chapbooks, *Thirst* and *Weather, Vistas, Houses, Dust.* His collection, *Shadow-Light,* was the Colorado Governor's Award volume in 1982. He lives in Denver, Colorado.

PAUL HUNTER's books include *Pullman* (University of Washington), *Mockingbird,* (Jawbone Press), and *It Loves Me It Loves Me Not* (Now It's Up To You Publications). He teaches high school in Seattle and is a musician and experienced sailor.

DAVID CHORLTON was born in Austria, and grew up in Manchester, England. His books include *Corn Dance* (Vienna), *No Mans' Land & Old Water* (Brushfire), *Allegiance to the Fire* (Bragdon Books) and *The Skin Beneath* (M.A.F. Press). He lives in Phoenix, Arizona.

HAROLD LITTLEBIRD is a widely published Native American poet. His most recent book is *On Mountains' Breath* (Tooth of Time). He received a Southwestern Association on Indian Affairs fellowship in 1983 and lives in Santa Fe.

SCOTT DAVIDSON received his MFA from the University of Montana in Missoula. His poems have appeared in *Cutbank, Pikestaff Forum, New Oregon Review,* and other magazines. He lives in Seattle.

BARBARA LA MORTICELLA edited *The Portland Poetry Festival Anthology* and co-edited *Confluence.* Her book of poetry is *Even the Hills Move in Waves* (Leaping Mountain). She lives in the hills outside Portland, Oregon.

CHRISTOPHER HOWELL's four books of poetry include *Sea Change* (L'Epervier'). He has been poetry editor for Lynx House Press since 1972. He is director of the Oregon Writers' Workshop in Portland and also works as a private investigator.

PATRICIA DUBRAVA's book of poetry is *Choosing the Moon* (Bread & Butter Press). She has been a contributing editor of *The Small Press Review* since 1976 and has had several plays produced in Denver, where she lives.

KARL KOPP's books of poetry include *Yarborough Mountain* (Baleen Press) and *The Juggler* (Place of Herons Press). He is co-publisher of Red Earth Press in Denver.

GRETEL EHRLICH's books are *To Touch the Water* (Ahsahta), *Geode/Rock Body* (Capra Press), *The Solace of Open Spaces* (Viking), and *City Tales, Wyoming Stories* (Capra). She lives on a ranch in Shell, Wyoming.

JOHN BRADLEY is co-publisher of Leaping Mountain Press in Fort Collins, Colorado. His book of poetry is *A-E-I-O-U* (Duluth Art Institute). He teaches English at Colorado State University.

TED KOOSER is author of five books of poetry, including *One World at a Time* (University of Pittsburgh). He is an underwriter in an insurance company in Lincoln, Nebraska.

JON DAVIS' first book of poetry, *Dangerous Amusements,* was published in 1987 by The Ontario Review Press. He has received fellowships from the NEA and The Fine Arts Work Center in Provincetown. He lives in Orange, Connecticut.

ALAN CHONG LAU's book of poetry is *Songs For Jadina* (Greenfield Review). Along with Lawson Inada and Garrett Hongo, he wrote *Budda Bandits Down Highway 99* (Buddhahead Press) and, with Mayuni Tsutakawa, co-edited *Turning Shadows Into Light* (Young Pine Press), an anthology of Asian American arts and culture. He lives in Seattle.

LEO ROMERO's books are *Agua Negra* (Ahsahta) and *Celso* (Arte Publico, the University of Houston). His poetry was adapted into a play by the Group Theater in Seattle in 1985. He lives in Santa Fe.

BETH BENTLEY's books of poetry are *Phone Calls From the Dead* and *Country of Resemblances* (both from Ohio University Press), and *The Purely Visible* (SeaPen Press). Ahsahta published her study of the poet Hazel Hall, an Oregon poet of the twenties. She lives in Seattle.

WENDY BARKER is the author of *Lunacy of Light: Emily Dickinson and The Experience of Metaphor* (Southern Illinois University). She was awarded an NEA grant in 1986 and teaches at the University of Texas in San Antonio.

TOM PARSON is publisher of Now It's Up To You Publications in Denver. He was one of the founders of Red Sky Poetry Theatre in Seattle, where he lived for many years. His poems have appeared in numerous magazines and anthologies.

DEL MARIE ROGER's chapbooks of poetry include *Breaking Free* (Ironwood Press), *To the Earth* (Trilobite Press), and *A Course in Dreams* (Mesilla Press). She has been a recipient of an NEA grant and lives in Rowlett, Texas.

KATHLEEN CAIN is a contributiong editor of *The Bloomsbury Review*. She received a writing fellowship from the Colorado Council On The Arts in 1984. Her books of poetry include *Self-Conscious* (Celtic Rose Press) and *1884: The First Year Out* (Mesilla Press). She lives in Denver.

JAMES HATHAWAY's book of poetry is *Foraging* (Ithaca House). He received an NEA fellowship in 1982 and a Pushcart Prize in poetry in 1986. He lives in Tempe, Arizona.

ROSEMARY CATACALOS' book of poetry, *Again For the First Time* (Tooth of Time), was awarded the Texas Institute of Letters Award in 1984, the same year she received their annual Dobie-Paisano Fellowship. She is Literature Director at the Guadalupe Arts Center in San Antonio.

LEROY QUINTANA's books of poetry include *Hijo del Pueblo: New Mexico Poems* (Puerto del Sol). He received an NEA fellowship in 1978 and is a marriage counselor in San Diego, California.

DON ERON received a writing fellowship from the Colorado Council On The Arts in 1984. His poetry has appeared in *The*

Ohio Review, Prairie Schooner, The Bloomsbury Review, and other magazines. He lives in Boulder, Colorado.

PHIL WOODS' poetry has appeared in *The Northwest Review, New Letters, The Bloomsbury Review,* and *City Kite On A Wire: 38 Denver Poets* (Mesilla Press). He has taught writing workshops at the Oregon State Penitentiary and lives in Denver. His chapbook of poems is *Waking the Woodcutter* (Leaping Mountain Press).

JUDITH SORNBERGER received her Ph.D. from the University of Nebraska. Her work has appeared in *Prairie Schooner, The Denver Quarterly, Tar River Poetry* and other publications. She lives in Littleton, Colorado.

BILL TREMBLAY's five books of poetry include *Second Sun: Selected and New Poems* (L'Epervier') and *Duhamel: Ideas of Order in Little Canada* (BOA Editions). He received an NEA grant in 1985 and teaches at Colorado State University in Fort Collins.

SANDRA CISNEROS' book of fiction, *The House On Mango Street* (Arte Publico), was awarded a 1985 Before Columbus American Book Award and she received a Texas Institute of Letters' Dobie-Paisano fellowship that same year. She divides her time between Illinois and Texas.

MICHAEL HOGAN has worked as a director of creative writing in Colorado prisons. His books of poetry include *The Broken Face of Summer* (Duck Down Press). He is director of legal research for an Arizona firm in Tucson.

CHARLES BEHLEN works as a house painter in San Antonio, while doing workshops for Poetry-In-The-Schools in Texas, New Mexico, and Arkansas. His books of poetry are *Perdition's Keepsake* (Prickly Pear Press) and *Dreaming at the Wheel* (Corona Press).

RAY GONZALEZ is poetry editor of *The Bloomsbury Review* in Denver and publisher of Mesilla Press. He edited *City Kite On A Wire: 38 Denver Poets* (Mesilla Press). His books of poetry are *From the Restless Roots* (Arte Publico), *Apprentice to Volcanos* (Leaping Mountain), and *Twilights and Chants* (James Andrews & Company).

GREG GLAZNER graduated from the writing program at the University of Montana in Missoula and received the Bess Hokin

Award from *Poetry* magazine. His chapbook of poetry is *Walking Two Landscapes* (State Street Press). He lives in Sante Fe.

RAYMOND CARVER's books of poems include *Where Water Comes Together With Other Water* and *Ultramarine* (both from Random House). He is a widely published fiction writer and received a Strauss Living Award in 1983. He lives in Port Angeles, Washington.

LONNY KANEKO's chapbook of poetry is *Coming Home From Camp* (Brooding Heron). He teaches at Highline College and lives on Vashon, an island in Puget Sound, Washington.

ARTHUR SZE's three books of poetry are *Dazzled* (Floating Island), *Two Ravens* and *The Willow Wind* (both from Tooth of Time). He has received an NEA grant and a Witter Bynner Foundation for Poetry Translation Grant. He lives in Santa Fe, where he teaches at the Institute of American Indian Arts.

LINDA HOGAN is a member of the Chickasaw Tribal Nation. She is the author of *Eclipse* (UCLA), and *Seeing Through the Sun* (University of Massachusetts). She received an NEA grant in fiction in 1986 and lives in Idledale, Colorado.

SAM HAMILL's most recent books are *Fatal Pleasure* and *The Nootka Rose* (both from Breitenbush). He has translated four books from the Chinese, one from the Latin of Catullus, and two from the Estonian of Jaan Kaplinski. He is publisher of Copper Canyon Press in Port Townsend, Washington.

JIM SIMMERMAN's book of poetry, *Home* (Dragon Gate), was a Pushcart Writer's Choice in 1983. He has been awarded fellowships from the NEA, the Arizona Commission on the Arts, and Bread Loaf. He teaches at Northern Arizona University in Flagstaff.

NANCY ANDREWS is the author of *Dimensions* (Graphic Impressions). Her work has appeared in *The Colorado State Review, The Wisconsin Review, The Bloomsbury Review,* and other magazines. She is the editor of James Andrews & Company in Golden, Colorado.

ALBERTO RIOS' first book of poetry, *Whispering To Fool The Wind* (Sheep Meadow Press) was awarded the Walt Whitman

Prize. His book of fiction, *The Iguana Killer* (Confluence) won the Western States Foundation Award. He teaches at Arizona State University in Tempe.

PAMELA USCHUK's chapbooks of poetry include *Light From Dead Stars* (Full Count Press) and *Loving the Outlaw* (Mesilla Press). She received an MFA from the University of Montana in Missoula where she edited *Cutbank.*

JANE KOPP is co-publisher of Red Earth Press in Denver. Her poetry has appeared in *City Kite On A Wire: 38 Denver Poets* (Mesilla Press).

MICHAEL SIMMS is the author of *Migration* (Breitenbush), a collection of poems, and the co-author, with Jack Myers, of the *Longman Dictionary and Handbook of Poetry* (Longman Publishers). He teaches at Southern Methodist University in Dallas, Texas.

WALTER PAVLICH's books of poetry are *Loadstones* (Mesilla Press), *Ongoing Portraits* (Barnwood), and *Of Things Odd And Therefore Beautiful* (Leaping Mountain). He lives in Davis, California.

MELINDA MUELLER's book of poetry, *Asleep In Another Country* (Jawbone Press) received a designation of Special Distinction from the Elliston Awards. She teaches high school biology in Seattle.

STANLEY NOYES is Literary Arts Coordinator for the New Mexico Arts Division in Santa Fe. His three books of poetry include *The Commander of Dead Leaves: A Dream Collection* (Tooth of Time).

JAMES GRABILL is co-publisher of Leaping Mountain Press in Fort Collins, Colorado. His books of poetry are *To Other Beings* (Lynx House), *Clouds Blowing Away* (Kayak Books), and *One River* (Momentum Press). He teaches at Colorado State University.

TESS GALLAGHER's three books of poetry are *Instructions To The Double, Under Stars,* and *Willingly* (all from Graywolf). Her book of short stories, *The Lover of Horses,* was published by Harper & Row in 1986. She lives in Port Angeles, Washington.

GENE FRUMPKIN's numerous books include *Clouds and Red Earth* (Swallow/Ohio University Press) and *A Lover's Quarrel With*

America (Automatic Press). He teaches at the University of New Mexico in Albuquerque.

FRANK STEWART's books of poetry are *The Open Water* and *Flying The Red Eye* (both from Floating Island) and *Reunion* (The Paper). He co-edited *Poetry Hawaii: A Contemporary Anthology* (University of Hawaii). He lives in Honolulu.